THE
TRUTH

DEDICATION

This book is dedicated with much love to my sister, Pamela, and to my nephews, Brad and Jeff.

THE FAITH SERIES

THE FAITH
Understanding Orthodox Christianity

THE WAY
*What Every Protestant Should Know
About the Orthodox Church*

THE TRUTH
*What Every Roman Catholic Should Know
About the Orthodox Church*

THE LIFE
The Orthodox Doctrine of Salvation

THE
TRUTH

What Every Roman Catholic Should Know
About the Orthodox Church

Clark Carlton

REGINA

SALISBURY, MA

1999

ISBN 0-9649141-8-2

Cover Photo: "Madonna" S. Apollinare Nuovo. Ravenna, Italy. Used by permission.

Appendix E, *The Tomus of 1285*, is included courtesy of Dr. Aristeides Papadakis and St. Vladimir's Seminary Press.

All Scripture Quotations are from the King James Version unless otherwise noted. Some quotations have been emended by the author to better reflect the original Greek text.

Regina Orthodox Press
PO Box 5288 Salisbury MA 01952 USA
Toll Free 800 636 2470
Fax 978 462 5079 non-USA 978 463 0730
www.reginaorthodoxpress.com

CONTENTS

APPENDICES

CONTENTS

ABOUT THE AUTHOR

Clark Carlton was born in Cookeville, Tennessee in 1964 and reared as a Southern Baptist. He earned a BA in philosophy from Carson-Newman College in Jefferson City, Tennessee. While studying as a Raymond Bryan Brown Memorial Scholar at the Southeastern Baptist Theological Seminary in Wake Forest, North Carolina, he converted to the Orthodox Faith and was chrismated at the St. Gregory the Great Orthodox Mission in Raleigh.

Mr. Carlton earned a Master of Divinity degree from St. Vladimir's Orthodox Theological Seminary in Crestwood, New York in 1990. His senior thesis, under the direction of Fr. John Meyendorff, was entitled "The Humanity of Christ According to St. Maximus the Confessor."

In 1993, he earned an MA in Early Christian Studies from the Catholic University of America in Washington, D.C. At present he is working as an adjunct instructor of philosophy at Tennessee Technological University in his home town while completing his Ph.D. dissertation on the dogmatic and ascetical theology of St. Mark the Monk (5th c.).

PREFACE

This book is the third installment in *The Faith Series* and the sequel to *The Way: What Every Protestant Should Know About the Orthodox Church*. Although *The Way* and *The Truth* are intended to be companion pieces, there is a significance difference between them. *The Way* was in large part autobiographical. My analysis of the differences between Orthodoxy and Protestantism was rooted in my own experience. My knowledge of Roman Catholicism, however, is entirely second-hand.

This means, of course, that I cannot offer the reader the depth of analysis I was able to provide in *The Way*. I understand Protestantism from the *inside*; I can only approach Roman Catholicism as an outsider. This enforced objectivity, however, is not without its benefits.

Almost all stories of recent Roman Catholic converts to Orthodoxy focus on Vatican II and the dissolution of the Church in which they were reared. While in no way wishing to dismiss the personal struggles of those who felt betrayed by the Vatican II Church, and not denying for a moment the fact that the Roman Catholic Church has become highly *protestantized* in the wake of Vatican II, the truth is that the *significant* changes in Roman Catholicism took place more than a millennium ago. The Roman Catholic Church of 1950 was no closer to Orthodoxy than is the Roman Catholic Church of today. This book, therefore, is a theological analysis of the differences between

Rome and Orthodoxy, not a critique of the reforms of Vatican II.

This book is intended primarily to give Roman Catholics a basic understanding of the Orthodox Church and the reasons why we are not in communion with one another. I trust, however, that it will also be of benefit to Orthodox Christians, who are often confused about the relationship of their Church to the Roman Catholic Church, and to Protestants, who are easily confused by the outward similarities between Orthodoxy and Roman Catholicism. For this reason, I have written an epilogue especially for Evangelical Protestants who are considering converting to the Roman Catholic Church.

Although the focus of this book is on the Orthodox Church, I found it necessary in places to describe in some detail the teachings of the Roman Catholic Church. In this case, comparison necessarily implies critique, for the Orthodox Church considers the Roman Catholic Church to be in heresy. I am fully aware that this may offend some readers. However, I can only beg the reader's indulgence, and ask that he or she approach this book with an open mind, knowing that truth has nothing to fear from free and open inquiry.

I would like to thank Archimandrite Damian and the brethren of the Monastery of the Glorious Ascension (Resaca, GA) for unlimited access to the monastery's library — about half of which seems to be lying about my study. I am also grateful to Dr. H. Tristram and Susan Engelhardt of Houston, Texas for their insight and encouragement. Finally, I am in the greatest debt to Mrs. Conrad (Mary) Stolzenbach and Mrs. Colin (Grace) Monk of St. Ignatius Orthodox Church in Franklin, TN for their assistance in proofreading the manuscript. Of course, all mistakes, whether typographical or substantive, are my responsibility alone.

Clark (Innocent) Carlton
Sunday of St. John of the Ladder
1999

Reverting, then, to that teaching which was common to the Churches of the East and of the West until the separation, we ought, with a sincere desire to know the truth, to search what the one, holy, catholic and orthodox apostolic Church of Christ, being then "of the same body," throughout the East and West believed, and to hold this fact entire and unaltered. But whatsoever has in later times been added or taken away, every one has a sacred and indispensable duty, if he sincerely seeks for the glory of God more than for his own glory, that in a spirit of piety he should correct it, considering that by arrogantly continuing in the perversion of the truth he is liable to a heavy account before the impartial judgment-seat of Christ (Encyclical of Patriarch Anthimos of Constantinople, 1895).

INTRODUCTION

Is Reunion Imminent?

Never, O Man, is that which concerns the Church put right through compromises: there is no mean between truth and falsehood. But just as what is outside the light will be necessarily in darkness, so also he who steps away a little from the truth is left subject to falsehood (St. Mark of Ephesus, †1443).

On October 21, 1997, Ecumenical Patriarch Bartholomeos received an honorary doctorate from Georgetown University in Washington, D.C. His speech was much anticipated by Roman Catholic clergy and scholars, who were expecting a major address on the state of Orthodox-Roman Catholic relations. Indeed, this is what they got, but the content of the patriarch's speech was far from what they expected.

While emphasizing his fervent desire for reconciliation between Rome and Orthodoxy ("Our heart is opposed to the specter of an everlasting separation"), Patriarch Bartholomeos stated,

> We confirm not with unexpected astonishment, but neither with indifference, that indeed (the divergence between us continually increases and the end point to which our courses are taking us, foreseeably, is indeed different.)

With these words, the Patriarch of Constantinople—
first among equals of the world's Orthodox episcopate—threw a bucket of ice water on the fervid hopes of
Roman Catholics that reunion with Orthodoxy could be
accomplished by the year 2000.[1]

To say that Roman Catholics were taken aback by
the patriarch's address would be an understatement. A
professor of mine from the Catholic University of
America called the remarks "insulting." Fr. Richard
John Neuhaus opined, "Bartholomew came and went,
and left in his wake a deeply dispirited company of
those who pray for reconciliation between East and
West."[2] He went on to say:

> The text of his speech was so virulently polemical
> that, at the urging of advisors, revisions were being
> made up until the last minute. But even then the fi-
> nal text offered naught for the comfort of those who
> were looking for a step forward.

The patriarch's Georgetown address and Fr.
Neuhaus' reaction to it provide an excellent starting
point for our study of Orthodox-Roman Catholic relations, affording us an opportunity to look beyond
popular assumptions and misconceptions and examine
the actual state of affairs. This book is subtitled, "What
Every Roman Catholic Should Know About the Orthodox Church." Perhaps the most important thing for

[1]The dawn of the next Christian millennium is an important
theme in Pope John Paul II's encyclical on Christian unity, *Ut
Unum Sint*.

[2]From Neuhaus' "Public Square" column in *First Things*
(March, 1988).

Roman Catholics to know is that much—if not most—of what they *think* they know about Orthodoxy is incorrect. Behind the disappointment of Fr. Neuhaus *et al.* lie several assumptions—assumptions held in common by most Roman Catholics. Before we examine in detail the major issues separating the Orthodox and Roman Catholic Churches, we must address these assumptions and explain why they are erroneous.

Doctrine and Politics

The first assumption often made by Roman Catholics is that there is virtually no real theological difference between the Orthodox and Roman Catholic Churches. In 1975, Pope Paul VI stated that Orthodox-Roman Catholic relations lack "little to attain the fullness that would permit a common celebration of the Lord's Eucharist."[3]

According to this assumption, what separates Rome and Orthodoxy is the exact role of the pope in the governance of the world-wide Church. The schism is, more or less, a political dispute. If, therefore, the pope is willing to make certain concessions in terms of his prerogatives, the Orthodox Church *should* then be able to once again recognize the primacy of the bishop of

---

[3]Quoted in the *Catechism of the Catholic Church,* English edition (Rome: Libreria Editrice Vaticana, 1994), §838, p. 222. Indeed, according to *Ut Unum Sint,* Pope Paul VI and the Second Vatican Council presuppose an already existing "communion of faith."

Rome, there being no real theological obstacles left to hurdle.[4]

The problem with this view is that it is not—and never has been—the view of the Orthodox Church. The governance of the Church is not and cannot be simply a matter of "church politics." Ecclesiology—the doctrine of the Church, including Her organization and government—is nothing else than the practical manifestation of Trinitarian and Christological doctrine. Differences in Church government, therefore, are inevitably manifestations of far more profound differences in theology. Such questions bear ultimately upon the very salvation of man, as Archimandrite Vasileios of Mt. Athos[5] says:

> Ecclesiology and spirituality have the same basis: dogma. The Church is Christ, His Body living in history. It is summarized in each of the faithful, who is the Church in miniature. The personal consciousness of each of the faithful has an ecclesial dimension, and every problem for the Church is the problem of the personal salvation of the faithful.[6]

The patriarch stressed this point in his Georgetown speech:

---

[4]This is Neuhaus' interpretation of *Ut Unum Sint*.

[5]Mt. Athos is the monastic republic on the Chalkidiki Peninsula in Greece. It is in many respects the spiritual heart of the Orthodox world.

[6]*Hymn of Entry*, Tr. by Elizabeth Briere (Crestwood, NY: SVS Press, 1984), pp. 20-21.

All this leads to the conclusion that the organization, the goals, the functions and all aspects of the
life of the Church are not determined by human
judgment, but the real and unchanging nature of
the Church. Thus, the steadfastness of the Orthodox
Church on ecclesiastical assumptions of every type
is not the product of any narrow perception, but the
natural result of our living ecclesiastical experience.
We are not talking about an object, subjected to our
free manipulation, but of an existence independent
of our desires and directed by Him who governs all
things and Who bestowed upon us limited responsibility or ministry.

This brings us to the heart of Patriarch Bartholomeos' remarks in Washington. What exactly did he
say that was so "virulently polemical"? The patriarch
stated,

Assuredly our problem is neither geographical nor
one of personal alienation. Neither is it a problem of
organizational structures, nor jurisdictional ar-
rangements. Neither is it a problem of external
submission, nor absorption of individuals and
groups. It is something deeper and more substantive.

The manner in which we exist has become onto-
logically different. Unless our ontological transfiguration and transformation toward one common
model of life is achieved, not only in form but also
in substance, unity and its accompanying realiza-
tion become impossible.

16

To put it another way, the Orthodox and Roman Catholic Churches have become expressions of two different faiths. Furthermore, the trajectory of these two faiths is neither parallel nor convergent, but divergent—moving further and further apart.

What Fr. Neuhaus interpreted as a virulent polemic was—from the standpoint of Patriarch Bartholomeos and the Orthodox Church—nothing more than an objective elucidation of the actual state of affairs. The patriarch did not openly call Roman Catholics "heretics," although one could reasonably draw that conclusion from his remarks. Even if he had, however, it would have been no more than Orthodox have said about Roman Catholics since the eleventh century.

The Development of Doctrine

The second erroneous assumption made by Roman Catholics is that Orthodox theology is as malleable as Roman Catholic theology has proven to be. Fr. Neuhaus speaks of Rome's willingness to change, and frankly expects the Orthodox to match this "progress":

> John Paul II has laid the foundation for the time when, as he has repeatedly said, "the Church will again breathe with both lungs, the East and the West." We must pray that one day the Orthodox will be prepared to join in building on that foundation.

What John Paul II has in fact done is to put a few of his papal prerogatives on the table for discussion. It is beyond dispute that the papacy has changed dramati-

cally over the years. (Few Roman Catholic scholars today would try to argue that early popes were considered either to be infallible or as possessors of universal
jurisdiction. If the papacy can change and accumulate
all kinds of authority, it can, by the same logic, divest
itself of some of those acquired powers when expediency demands it.)

The problem, from an Orthodox point of view, is
that ecclesiology is not subject to change. If Christ had
truly willed that the bishop of Rome be His vicar on
earth, exercising not only infallibility but also immediate and ordinary jurisdiction over the entire Church,
then this state of affairs must have existed from the beginning, and it certainly cannot be up for negotiation.)

In short, the doctrine of the papacy is either di-
vinely revealed dogma or it is heresy.) It is not an issue,
however, in which both sides can make a few concessions. To repeat, basic ecclesiological doctrine is not up
for revision.)

The Orthodox position on this matter is quite simple: the Roman Catholic doctrine of the papacy represents a radical departure from the ecclesiology of the
early Church. In short, it is a heresy. Union between
Rome and Orthodoxy requires not that the pope make a
few concessions in regard to his (relatively) recently acquired prerogatives, but that he repent of his heresy
and wholeheartedly return to the Orthodox Catholic
Faith, which the Orthodox Church holds now and has
held since Pentecost.

To reiterate: the differences between the Orthodox
and Roman Catholic Churches are primarily neither

cultural nor political, but theological. We simply do not confess the same faith. Furthermore, the theology of the Orthodox Church is not up for negotiation. Under the cover of "the development of doctrine," Roman Catholic theology has changed frequently and often dramatically through the centuries. It will, no doubt, change again and again as the years progress. It is a grave mistake, however, to assume that Orthodox theology will also change in order to meet Rome "half way."

The "Dialogue of Love"

This is not to suggest that there are no Orthodox who are willing to reconsider matters of doctrine in order to secure the much sought after "reunion of Churches." There certainly are, and many of them are in the forefront of the ecumenical movement. This brings us to the third erroneous assumption often made by Roman Catholics in regard to Orthodoxy, namely, that those who participate in ecumenical dialogues are truly representative—in either a juridical or a more general, moral sense—of the Orthodox Church as a whole.

One cannot really blame Fr. Neuhaus for his reaction to the patriarch's address. After all, patriarchs of Constantinople have been making positive—some would say fawning—overtures to Rome since the 1960's. Furthermore, there have been enough dialogues and "agreed statements" over the last three decades to heighten anyone's anticipation. Indeed, Patriarch Bartholomeos' Georgetown address seems oddly out of character with previous statements.

What, then, are we to make of this apparent discrepancy? Does the ecumenical patriarch speak for the Orthodox Church or not? Furthermore, are we to heed the patriarch who speaks of Rome and Orthodoxy as "Sister Churches" and "two lungs" of the same body, or the patriarch who speaks of Rome and Orthodoxy as manifesting two different ontologies?

First of all, the ecumenical patriarch does *not* speak for the Orthodox Church in the same way that the pope can be said to speak for the Roman Church. There is a tendency among Westerners to think of the patriarch as a sort of Orthodox pope, but this is based on ignorance, not fact.

The second question is more difficult to answer. However, rather than asking which position represents Patriarch Bartholomeos' *true* opinion on the question of reunion with Rome, we should ask which position represents the true opinion of the Orthodox Church as a whole. In the final analysis, the opinion of Bartholomeos—even as ecumenical patriarch—matters little. What matters is the mind of the Church, Her "catholic consciousness."

That question is much easier to answer. I have appended to this book three documents pertaining to Orthodox-Roman Catholic relations. These documents range in date from 1994 to 1285. The first document is actually a letter of protest written to Patriarch Bartholomeos in regard to the "Balamand Statement"—precisely the kind of ecumenical overture toward Rome that Fr. Neuhaus finds so encouraging. If you read these documents carefully, you will find that the patriarch's Georgetown comments are in keeping with the other documents.

In contrast, a good deal of the rhetoric issuing from the "dialogue of love" between Orthodoxy and Rome is blatantly contrary to the position the Orthodox have consistently held since the eleventh/twelfth centuries. Let us take, for example, the expression "Sister Churches." Since the reign of Patriarch Athenagoras in the 1960's, patriarchs have repeatedly referred to Rome as a "Sister Church." Pope John Paul II has made much of this term, noting its antiquity.[7] Surely, however, both pope and patriarch realize that in the ancient Church such terminology was used by Churches *in communion* with one another. No one would have dared to use the term in reference to the Arians or Nestorians. In other words,/the term "Sister Churches" implies a degree of

---

[7]"In each local Church this mystery of divine love is enacted, and surely this is the ground of the traditional and very beautiful expression 'Sister Churches', which local Churches were fond of applying to one another (cf. Decree, Unitatis Redintegratio, 14). For centuries we lived this life of 'Sister Churches', and together held Ecumenical Councils which guarded the deposit of faith against all corruption. And now, after a long period of division and mutual misunderstanding, the Lord is enabling us to discover ourselves as 'Sister Churches' once more, in spite of the obstacles which were once raised between us. If today, on the threshold of the third millennium, we are seeking the re-establishment of full communion, it is for the accomplishment of this reality that we must work and it is to this reality that we must refer." *Ut Unum Sint*, 57.

theological unity between Rome and Orthodoxy that simply does not exist.)

Another example of inflated, ecumenical rhetoric is the statement that East and West are the "two lungs" of the Church. The use of this expression—also a favorite of John Paul II—is even more bizarre than referring to the Roman Catholic and Orthodox Churches as "Sisters." It is a flat denial of the very definition of the Church as *catholic*.

Contrary to popular opinion, the word *catholic* does *not* mean "universal"; it means "whole, complete, lacking nothing." This misunderstanding goes back at least to the time of St. Augustine. Thus, to confess the Church to be *catholic* is to say that She possesses the fullness of the Christian faith. To say, however, that Orthodoxy and Rome constitute two lungs of the same Church is to deny that either Church separately is catholic in any meaningful sense of the term. This is not only contrary to the teaching of Orthodoxy, it is flatly contrary to the teaching of the Roman Catholic Church, which considers itself truly catholic.[8]

The use of phrases such as "Sister Churches" and "two lungs" should be of as much concern to conservative Roman Catholics as to the Orthodox. Taken seriously, they imply that neither the Orthodox nor the Roman Catholic Church considers itself to be complete without the other. No council of the Orthodox Church

---

[8]The catholicity, i.e. fullness, of the Roman Catholic Church is affirmed in *Lumen Gentium* and in *Ut Unum Sint*.

and no council of the Roman Catholic Church—not even Vatican II—has ever asserted such a thing.

I emphasize this point because Fr. Neuhaus would have us believe that the Orthodox opponents of the reunion of the "two lungs" of the Church are a "revanchist" element, opposing unity out of spite. On the contrary, the monks of Mt. Athos and the other Orthodox critics of the modern ecumenical movement are merely pointing out the *fact* that the very definition of the Church as *catholic* precludes the possibility of there being *another* catholic Church.

If the rhetoric of "Sister Churches" and "the two lungs of the Church" is so foreign to the stated ecclesiology of *both* the Roman Catholic and Orthodox Churches—both considering themselves to be *the* Catholic Church—why do people continue to use it? More to the point, why do bishops and other clergy use it?

To find out why some Orthodox have used this language we need look no further than the text of the most famous—or infamous—"agreed statement" signed by members of the Roman Catholic and Orthodox Churches. The "Balamand Statement" was issued by the Joint International Commission for the Theological Dialogue between the Roman Catholic Church and the Orthodox Church, VIIth Plenary Session, Balamand School of Theology (Lebanon), 17-24 June, 1993.[9]

[9]For the full text of the Balamand Statement see the *Eastern Churches Journal*, vol. 1, No. 1. The reader should note that this statement, although signed by the representatives of several (but not all) Orthodox Churches, has no "official" standing. It has never

INTRODUCTION

The purpose of the Balamand Conference was to discuss the problem of *Uniatism*. Also known as Byzantine or Eastern Rite Catholicism, Uniatism refers to Churches under the authority of Rome that use Eastern liturgical practices and (at least in theory) Eastern canon law.[10] Originating in the sixteenth century,[11] Uniatism has been a powerful force—and a major thorn in the side of the Orthodox Church—in many parts of the world, most critically in Eastern Europe and the Middle East.

[Roman Catholics have tended to view Uniatism as a step toward unity. The Orthodox, on the other hand, have always seen it as a manifestation of Rome's desire not to unite with the Orthodox Church, but to subjugate Her.)Indeed,/most of the so-called "unions" of Eastern Christians with Rome (actually *under* Rome) were imposed on a less-than-willing populace through the use of secular force.)It is against this background that we must understand the following:

12) Because of the way in which Catholics and Orthodox once again consider each other in relation-

been formally approved by any Orthodox Church. I have appended a letter of protest from the Monks of Mt. Athos to Ecumenical Patriarch Bartholomeos in regard to the Balamand Statement (Appendix A). For an additional critique, see John Romanides' article in *Theologia* [The periodical of the Church of Greece] VI:3 (1993), pp. 570-580.

[10]Uniates usually insist that they are "in communion" with Rome, not under the rule of Rome. This, however, is a purely semantic distinction, with no basis in reality.

[11]For a brief historical overview, see Timothy (Kallistos) Ware, *The Orthodox Church* (New York: Penguin Books, 1984), pp. 103ff.

ship to the mystery of the Church and discover each other once again as Sister Churches, this form of "missionary apostolate" described above, and which has been called "uniatism", can no longer be accepted either as a method to be followed nor as a model of the unity our Churches are seeking.

For the most part, the Orthodox Churches throughout the world are in a state of material need. There is simply no way they can match the vast resources that Rome is able to muster. The Orthodox, therefore, feel threatened by the prospect of renewed proselytism on the part of the materially affluent and politically well connected Roman Church.[12]

The reasoning behind the Balamand Statement takes the form of an extended hypothetical syllogism: 1) If Rome believes herself to be the only true Church, she will strive to bring the Orthodox Church under her control. 2) If Rome strives to bring the Orthodox Church under her control, she will use her vast material superiority to accomplish the task. 3) If Rome uses her vast material superiority to proselytize the Orthodox, then tens of thousands, if not millions, will leave the Orthodox Church and come under the authority of Rome.

---

[12]These fears are not without foundation. The Fatima "prophecies" — believed by millions of Roman Catholics, including Pope John Paul II--have given rise to a new impetus within the Roman Catholic Church for the "evangelization" of Russia. In particular, the "Second Secret" of Fatima states that a period of worldwide peace will ensue if Russia is "consecrated to the Immaculate Heart of Mary." The so-called prophecy predicts dire consequences if this does not happen. We shall return to the Fatima "prophecies" below.

The Balamand Statement asserts, however, that since Rome no longer sees herself as the only Church — the Orthodox and Roman Catholic Churches having come to see each other as "Sisters" — there is now no impetus for her to proselytize the Orthodox, especially using the tool of uniatism. The problem is that such reasoning constitutes a logical fallacy.[13] Use of the term "Sister Church" does not *necessarily* imply that Rome will no longer seek to bring the Orthodox under her control. Indeed, as long as the Roman Church defines subjection to the pope as a criterion of being in the one Catholic Church[14], then such attempts are inevitable.[15]

It is evident from the foregoing that Orthodox participation in ecumenical dialogues is usually done from a standpoint of material and political weakness. Thus,

[13]The argument may be expressed in this way: If Rome believes herself to be the only true Church (R), she will strive to bring the Orthodox Church under her control (O). Rome no longer believes herself to be the only Church (~R). Therefore, Rome will no longer strive to bring the Orthodox Church under her control (~O). Expressed symbolically: R>O / ~R // ~O. This is a formal logical fallacy known as "denying the antecedent."

[14]Cf. *Lumen Gentium:* "This Church constituted and organized in the world as a society, subsists in the Catholic Church, which is governed by the successor of Peter and by the Bishops in communion with him ..." (§8). And: "They are fully incorporated in the society of the Church who, possessing the Spirit of Christ accept her entire system and all the means of salvation given to her, and are united with her as part of her visible bodily structure and through her with Christ, who rules her through the Supreme Pontiff and the bishops" (§14).

[15]Indeed, Rome has done nothing to discourage the Unia, nor has she invited any of the "Eastern Catholic Churches" to return to their Orthodox mother Churches.

statements such as the one signed at Balamand are occasioned primarily by *political* motivations. As such, the *theological* implications of the statements are not always well thought out.[16]

The bottom line is this: If you want to understand the true nature of Orthodox-Roman Catholic relations, do not begin with politically motivated statements such as the Balamand Statement. (Orthodox theology is not determined by academics or committees of "experts." On the contrary, it is in the bosom of the Church, particularly the monasteries, where one finds the most authentic witness to the Orthodox experience.) In this book, I have tried to be faithful to that witness in presenting the differences between the Orthodox and Roman Catholic Churches.

---

[16]Fr. Neuhaus notes that "friends of unity" in the Orthodox Church have suggested that Patriarch Bartholomeos' Georgetown address was politically motivated — being aimed at placating conservative critics — and that terms such as "ontological" need not be taken seriously. Fortunately, Fr. Neuhaus has enough acumen to realize that this "has the appearance of grasping at straws." Indeed, I would argue that it is precisely the language of "Sister Churches" that constitutes "empty rhetoric" on the part of the Orthodox and that the patriarch's Georgetown statement should be given full theological consideration. It is the latter, not the former that is in conformity with Orthodox tradition.

Holy Romans and Byzantine Intrigue

Because those things that are ours were once venerable to the Westerns, as having the same divine Offices and confessing the same Creed; but the novelties were not known to our Fathers, nor could they be shown in the writings of the orthodox Western Fathers, nor as having their origin either in antiquity or catholicity. Moreover, neither Patriarchs nor Councils could then have introduced novelties amongst us, because the protector of religion is the very body of the Church, even the people themselves, who desire their religious worship to be ever unchanged and of the same kind as that of their fathers (Encyclical of the Eastern Patriarchs, 1848).

There is an old joke, much beloved of high-school history teachers, that states that the Holy Roman Empire was neither holy nor Roman. From an Orthodox perspective, the same joke—though it is no laughing matter—could be applied to the Roman Catholic Church. That is, the Roman Church is neither Roman nor catholic. Indeed, from the crowning of Charlemagne in AD 800, the destinies of the Holy

Roman Empire and the Roman Catholic Church were so inextricably intertwined that the destiny of one necessarily affected the destiny of the other.[1]

This, of course, will come as a great surprise to most Roman Catholics. After all, the Roman Catholic Church is the largest religious organization in the world, a worldwide bureaucracy headed by the most famous and most powerful religious leader in the world. How could the Church that has always resided in Rome not be Roman?[2] How could a universal religious organization not be catholic? To answer these questions, we must *unlearn* a great deal of what we have been taught about Christian history and divest ourselves of prejudices that have been continually reinforced by less-than-thorough historians.

For Roman Catholics, Rome is the center of the ecclesiastical universe and always has been. The Roman Church is *the* Catholic Church, that is, the Church that is spread out to all corners of the world, the *universal* Church. Latin is—or was, until Vatican II—the universal liturgical language. The Latin Mass is the universally accepted eucharistic rite.

There are other "Churches," of course, either subsets of the Roman Catholic Church like the Uniates

---

[1]The Holy Roman Empire is occasionally dated from the coronation of Otto I in 962. While it is true that the Carolingian Empire fell into disarray after the death of Charlemagne, there can be no question that Charlemagne set the stage for what was to come after him. For this reason, I feel justified in dating the Holy Roman Empire from his reign.

[2]Keep in mind that for 70 years following 1309 popes resided not in Rome, but in Avignon, as tools of the French crown.

or in schism from Rome like the Orthodox. These are ethnic Churches, old, venerable, somewhat exotic, but definitely outside the norm, subservient to the standard Roman usage. After all, the pope—the sole head of the universal Church and the Vicar of Christ on earth—celebrates the Roman Mass in Latin.

A Rose by Any Other Name

This jaundiced view of the world rests upon a false dichotomy that is so well ingrained in our thinking that even Orthodox accept it without hesitation: the Roman Empire and Church *vs.* the Byzantine Empire and Church. Before we do anything else, therefore, we must disabuse ourselves of this false dichotomy.

Let me state this as clearly and succinctly as possible: there has never at any time in the world's history been a *Byzantine Empire*. When, after his conversion, St. Constantine rebuilt the town of Byzantium as his new imperial residence and capital, renaming it Constantinople, he did not thereby create a new empire. Although the imperial administration subsequently shifted from Rome to Constantinople—New Rome—the empire remained one and the same.[3]

---

[3]According to A.H.M. Jones, Constantinople was originally conceived as more of an imperial residence than a capital. The senate, which was dominated by pagans well into the fifth century, remained in Rome. Eventually a senate was created in Constantinople as well, though it was of a very different character from the one in old Rome, dominated as it was by the old Roman aristocracy. Far from being antithetical to the policies of the emperor, the Constantinopolitan senate was composed in part by

For centuries, historians have taught us that the Roman Empire began to decline with the sack of Rome in 410 by the Goths. While this event sent shockwaves throughout Western Europe and North Africa, it was hardly noticed in Constantinople.[4] Why? Because even if the *city* of Rome had fallen to the barbarians, the *Roman Empire* was still intact and functioning. Jones makes the point:

> All the historians who have discussed the decline and fall of the Roman empire have been Westerners. Their eyes have been fixed on the collapse of Roman authority in the Western parts and the evolution of the medieval Western European world. They have tended to forget, or brush aside, one very important fact, that the Roman empire, though it may have declined, did not fall in the fifth century nor indeed for another thousand years.[5]

If the empire centered in Constantinople was the same as the old Roman Empire, where did the name "Byzantine" come from? More to the point, why has it been so universally accepted and why does it really matter?

---

imperial administrators and worked in conjunction with imperial policy. *The Later Roman Empire 284-602: A Social, Economic, and Administrative Survey,* Vol. 1 (Baltimore: Johns Hopkins Univ. Press, 1990), pp. 83-84, 132-133.

[4]For the reaction to the sack of Rome among Latin writers, see Jones, Vol. 2, p. 1025.

[5]Jones, Vol. 2, pp. 1026-1027.

The word "Byzantine" is quite ancient, and even after the name of Byzantium was changed to Constantinople, people occasionally used it to designate the inhabitants of the city. It was not, however, used to refer to the empire itself or to its citizens living outside the precincts of the imperial city. On the contrary, the citizens of the "Byzantine Empire" referred to themselves as "Romans" because they were citizens of the Roman Empire.[6]

Even after the Moslem Conquest, the Christians living in the Moslem territories were called Romans. Indeed, according to Moslem law, all Christians living in Moslem territory, regardless of race or language, were said to comprise the *Rum Millet,* or Roman nation. To this day, the official address of the Patriarch of Constantinople is the *Rum Patrikhanesi,* the Roman Patriarchate.

What historians occasionally refer to as the restoration of the Western Empire by Charlemagne was viewed by the Roman imperial court in Constantinople

---

[6]For evidence based on coinage, see Clifton R. Fox, "What, if Anything, is a Byzantine," *Celator* 10:3 (March, 1996). Fox is incorrect, however, when he states that the late Romans did not know the term "Byzantine." Keep in mind that the Roman Empire, unlike other ancient empires, extended citizenship to the peoples they conquered. St. Paul, for example, was a Roman citizen, even though he was a Middle-Eastern Jew (cf. Acts 22:25 ff.). The Roman Empire was a multi-ethnic, multi-national, multi-linguistic reality. Thus, the Roman citizens of Asia Minor were just as much Roman citizens as the citizens of the Eternal City.

as a usurpation.[7] Although the Roman court had to come to terms with Charlemagne for political reasons, it never trusted the Frankish (Germanic) Empire established by Charlemagne. Significantly, Charlemagne, who tried to claim the mantle of the Roman Empire for himself, referred to the citizens under the Roman emperor of Constantinople not as Romans, but as "Greeks."[8]

Thus, under Charlemagne, a false dichotomy was posited whereby the "Roman Empire" of Western Europe was juxtaposed against the "Greek Empire" in Constantinople. In reality, however, Charlemagne's empire centered at Aix-la-Chapelle had nothing to do with Rome, except that he was able to exert enough pressure on the pope to be crowned emperor by papal hands.[9] The empire in Constantinople, on the other

[7]Cf. Francis Dvornik, *Byzantium and the Roman Primacy* (New York: Fordham Univ. Press, 1966), p. 116. Hereafter cited as *Byzantium.*

[8]This usage was to become commonplace throughout the West: "An incident that took place in 968 shows how little these newcomers understood the idea of a universal empire in which Byzantium believed so strongly. That year, Otto I sent a Lombard who knew Greek, Liutprand of Cremona, to the Emperor Nicephoras Phocas, to ask of him the hand of the Byzantine Princess for his son, the future Emperor. Pope John XII, recommending the ambassador to the Emperor, called Nicephorus 'Emperor of the Greeks.' He could have hardly offered a more striking insult to the Byzantines who thought of themselves as Romans." Dvornik, *Byzantium,* p. 126.

[9]As one historian put it, "The man who came to Rome in 800 to be crowned came as a conqueror, not as a suppliant." Peter Gay

hand, was the historical continuation of the Roman Empire.

While Charlemagne's use of "Greek" to describe the Eastern Roman Empire was, no doubt, meant to bolster his own claims to the mantle of Rome, it had the additional effect of being highly insulting to the Christians of the empire. By this time, the adjective "Greek" had become synonymous with "pagan." In fact, the Church officially condemned those who followed the "*hellenic* myths."[10]

It was not until the modern period that people began to refer to the Eastern Roman Empire as the Byzantine Empire. The first to do so may have been the sixteenth-century German historian Hieronymous Wolf. He was followed in this by the great, seventeeth-century French historian Charles DuCange. Today, the term "Byzantine Empire" is so ubiquitous, it is rare to find the Eastern Roman Empire referred to as anything

and R.K. Webb, *Modern Europe to 1815* (New York: Harper and Row, 1973), p. 28.

[10]The linguistic identification of Greek with pagan can already be found in the New Testament, where it can sometimes be translated as Gentile (as opposed to Jew) or even heathen. In late antiquity, the Greek speaking Orthodox were very conscious of the Greek philosophical tradition and the dangers it posed for Christian theology. This contributed to their reluctance to identify themselves as Greeks. See St. Athanasius the Great's *Discourse Against the Greeks*, which appears in *the Nicene and Post Nicene Fathers* (Series 2, Vol. 4) as *Against the Heathen*. For a brief overview of the relation between Orthodox theology and Hellenistic philosophy see J. Meyendorff, "Greek Philosophy and Christian Theology in the Early Church," in *Catholicity and the Church* (Crestwood, NY: SVS Press, 1983), pp. 31-47.

other than Byzantine. Even scholars who know that the term is technically incorrect continue to use it.[11]

The Orthodox scholar Fr. John Romanides sees the use of the term "Byzantine" as a deliberate continuation of Charlemagne's propaganda campaign.[12] While I certainly do not subscribe to Fr. Romanides' conspiracy theories, it can hardly be denied that the use of the term has had the same practical effect as Charlemagne's use of the term "Greek," namely to direct attention away from the fundamental *discontinuity* between the Germanic "Holy Roman Empire" and the real Roman Empire.[13] At the same time, it clouds the fundamental *identity* between the empire centered in Constantinople and the empire of old Rome.[14]

[11]This applies to Orthodox scholars as well. Several studies by Orthodox writers quoted in this work have "Byzantine" in their titles. Although Fr. John Meyendorff used the term "Byzantine" freely, he was well aware that the inhabitants of the empire knew themselves to be Romans.

[12]John S. Romanides, *Franks, Romans, Feudalism and Doctrine* (Brookline, MA: Holy Cross Orthodox Press, 1981). The reader should be warned that Romanides' work is rife with conspiracy theories. One does not have to agree with all of Romanides' theories, however, in order to appreciate the basic facts that he marshals in regard to the identity of the *real* Roman Empire.

[13]According to Dvornik, "Less and less did the Westerners understand the Byzantine concept of a universal Christian Empire and in the West, the idea that only the Emperor crowned by the Pope in Rome was the true successor of the Caesars began to receive general acceptance. The existence of a Roman Emperor in Constantinople had all but faded from memory." *Byzantium*, p. 127.

[14]There is one other reason for refraining from calling the Roman Empire the Byzantine Empire. "Byzantine" has come to have negative connotations in modern parlance. The word has

CHAPTER ONE

Franks, Romans, Countrymen

You may well ask at this point what any of this has
to do with Orthodox-Roman Catholic relations. Its
relevance lies in the influence that the Frankish Empire
was to exert on the Church of Rome, an influence that
would eventually lead to the schism between Rome and
the Orthodox Churches of the East.

Although barely literate himself, Charlemagne
fancied himself a patron of the arts and learning and
assembled a team of scholars at his court.[15] When it

become synonymous with labyrinthine complexity, corruption, and
political intrigue. However, these words could be equally applied
to any court—ecclesiastical or political—in the ancient world.
Indeed the turmoil in the papal court of the tenth century rivals
anything that took place in Constantinople: "In 904, Sergius III had
his two rivals, Leo V and Christopher I, incarcerated and killed. He
had come to power with the support of one of the most powerful
families in Italy. This family was headed by Theophylact and his
wife Theodora, whose daughter, Marozia, was Sergius' lover.
Shortly after the death of Sergius, Marozia and her husband Guido
of Tuscia captured the Lateran palace and made John X their
prisoner, subsequently suffocating him with a pillow. After the
brief pontificates of Leo VI and Stephen VII, Marozia placed on the
papal throne, with the name of John XI, the son whom she had had
from her union with Sergius III. Thirty years after the death of John
XI, that papacy was in the hands of John XII, a grandson of
Marozia. Later, her nephew became John XIII. His successor,
Benedict VI, was overthrown and strangled by Crescentius, a
brother of John XIII. John XIV died of either poison or starvation in
the dungeon where he had been thrown by Boniface VII, who in
turn was poisoned." Justo J. González, *The Story of Christianity*, Vol.
1 (New York: Harper & Row, 1984), p. 275.

[15]"The intellectual eminence of his reign is a comment on the
flatness of the surrounding landscape; still, scholars from all across

came to the subject of theology, however, the Frankish court and its theologians were utterly incompetent.[16] This incompetence was to prove fatal for Christian unity. Let us consider two examples of the Frankish theological program.

During the eighth and ninth centuries, the Eastern Roman Empire was rocked by the iconoclastic controversy. The use of icons was condemned as idolatry. In 787, a council was held at Constantinople at which the use of icons was declared to be not only acceptable, but necessary if one was to maintain a correct understanding of Christology. That is, icons were deemed to be a theological witness to the fact that in Christ, the invisible God, had made Himself visible. The fathers made a clear distinction between the relative veneration (*proskinesis*) given to icons (the honor of which passes to the person depicted) and worship (*latreia*), which is offered to God alone.[17]

Europe flocked to his court at Aix-la-Chapelle." Gay and Webb, p. 28.

[16]"The most serious consequence of the creation of Charlemagne's empire was the appearance of a new type of Christianity in the West, the work of men from the 'barbarian' parts of Northern Europe, who were only very vaguely acquainted with the intellectual atmosphere of the Roman-Byzantine world in which the Fathers of the Church had lived and in which the ancient councils had been held." John Meyendorff, *The Orthodox Church: Its Past and Its Role in the World Today* (Crestwood, NY: SVS Press, 1981), p. 43. Cited hereafter as *Orthodox Church*.

[17]The relevant primary sources for the Orthodox theory of icons are readily available in English. See St. John of Damascus, *On the Divine Images*, David Anderson, tr. (Crestwood, NY: SVS Press,

Although the issue was not finally settled until the ninth century, this council came to be accepted in both the East and the West as the Seventh Ecumenical Council—accepted everywhere, that is, except in the Frankish Empire. In 792, Charlemagne sent the *Libri Carolini*—ostensibly written by himself, but most certainly written by someone else—to the pope. The *Caroline Books* contained the Frankish refutation of the Seventh Council. In a stupendous display of ignorance, the author actually accused the "Greeks" of authorizing the worship, or "superstitious adoration," of icons.[18]

Far more important than the Franks' bizarre interpretation of the iconoclast controversy, however, was their championing of the addition of a word to the Nicene Creed: the *Filioque*. This word, meaning "and the Son," was inserted into the clause on the Holy Spirit, affirming that the Spirit proceeds from the Second Person of the Trinity as well as from the Father. We shall discuss the *Filioque* and the doctrine of the Trinity in detail below. For the moment, let us note that the Frankish theologians became the primary promoters of this addition.[19]

What is really amusing is that Charlemagne's theologians, who had displayed their ignorance so

1980) and St. Theodore the Studite, *On the Holy Icons*, Catharine P. Roth, tr. (Crestwood, NY: SVS Press, 1981).

[18]Cf. Jaroslav Pelikan, *The Christian Tradition: A History of the Development of Doctrine*, Vol. 2, *The Spirit of Eastern Christendom (600-1700)* (Chicago: University of Chicago Press, 1977), p. 156. Cited hereafter as *Spirit*.

[19]The *Filioque* is also a major topic of the *Libri Carolini*. Cf. Meyendorff, *Orthodox Church*, p. 42.

brilliantly with their statements on the Seventh
Ecumenical Council, outdid themselves in regard to the
Filioque: they actually accused the "Greeks" of *removing*
the novel word from the original creed! At this point we
should stress that the Nicene Creed—like the New
Testament itself—was written in Greek. Greek, not
Latin, was the language in which Christian dogma was
originally formulated.[20] All of the Ecumenical Councils
took place in the East. Their deliberations, as well as
their decisions, were in Greek. Even when letters from
the pope were circulated in the East, they were read in
Greek translation, with the translators occasionally
taking liberties with the text.[21]

I belabor this point to stress the fact Rome was *never*
the center of Christian theological formulation. This is
not to suggest that popes and Roman theologians

[20]In fact, Greek was the original language of the Roman
Church. *I Clement*, the oldest extant papal document (c. AD 96),
was written in Greek. Indeed, it was not until the third century that
Latin became commonly used by popes and Roman theologians.
Cf. Johannes Quasten, *Patrology*, Vol. 2, *The Ante-Nicene Literature
After Irenaeus* (Westminster, MD: Christian Classics, Inc., 1986), pp.
153ff. Many Greek speakers argued that Latin was incapable of the
subtleties of theological and philosophical thought. The Emperor
Michael III, for example, referred to Latin as a "barbaric" and
"Scythian" tongue. Though it may sound contentious and
parochial, there is some justification for the comment. Until the
advent of Christian philosophy with St. Augustine and Boethius,
very little serious philosophy had been written in Latin. Cicero
dabbled in philosophy, but his originality has been called into
serious question. The Emperor Marcus Aurelius, arguably the most
able philosopher of his day, wrote in Greek.
[21]Cf. Pelikan, *Spirit*, p. 155.

played no role in the formulation of doctrine, but rather to underscore the fact that it was never a central role. Even the *Tome of [Pope] Leo*, so influential at the Council of Chalcedon, was interpreted in light of the theology of St. Cyril of Alexandria, who was the touchstone of orthodoxy for the Fathers of that council.[22]

The Frankish theologians, therefore, had the whole matter of the *Filioque* upside down. It was not the Eastern Romans—whose forebears had written the creed, in Greek—who had deleted the phrase from the creed. Rather, it was the Franks themselves who were pushing a novelty, in Latin. Significantly, popes resisted this addition until the eleventh century. In 809, for example, Pope Leo III refused Charlemagne's request to sing the *Filioque* in the creed.[23] Leo even had the creed inscribed, without the *Filioque*, on silver plaques.

For the most part, popes arbitrated between the Frankish and East Roman Empires and Churches. Pope Nicholas I (858-867), however, decided to take advantage of political divisions among the Franks and instability within the East Roman court to press his own claims for universal jurisdiction. What followed was a running feud between Rome and Constantinople known to history as the "Photian Schism." During this controversy, Popes Nicholas I and Hadrian II argued

[22]Cf. John Meyendorff, *Imperial Unity and Christian Divisions: The Church 450-680 A.D.* (Crestwood, NY: SVS Press, 1989), pp. 171-178. Cited hereafter as *Imperial Unity*.

[23]Pelikan, *Spirit*, pp. 186-187. Leo stated that he did not have a problem with the *Filioque*, but he was not about to unilaterally change the Nicene Creed.

with Patriarch Photius of Constantinople over the nature of the authority of the Roman Church and the *Filioque.*[24]

The schism was healed at a reunion council held in Constantinople in 879. At that council, legates of Pope John VIII (872-882) signed the condemnation of any "additions" to the Nicene Creed and of anyone who denied the legitimacy of the Seventh Ecumenical Council and its decree on icons. Furthermore, the Sees of Old and New Rome agreed not to interfere in each other's internal affairs. This council was confirmed by Pope John VIII and was regarded in Rome as the Eighth Ecumenical Council...until the eleventh century.

The Council of 879 is of incalculable importance. Not only did it heal the "Photian Schism," it set official Roman Catholic policy on the issues of controversy with the East. First of all, the addition of the *Filioque* to the creed was flatly condemned. Second, the affirmation of the Seventh Council could have only been directed at the Frankish theologians, who had objected to the council. Finally, by agreeing not to interfere in the internal matters of the See of Constantinople, the Pope tacitly rejected any claim of universal jurisdiction. Thus, at the end of the ninth century, communion between Rome and Constantinople was restored, with Rome flatly rejecting the theological novelties and jurisdictional claims that

[24]For a brief description of the events see Meyendorff, *Orthodox Church*, pp. 39ff. For a more detailed study see Francis Dvornik, *The Photian Schism: History and Legend* (Cambridge, Cambridge University Press, 1948).

would eventually drive the two Churches apart...in the eleventh century.[25]

The Reformation of the Eleventh Century

One of the most significant byproducts of Frankish hegemony in Western Europe was the fact that the Western Church was almost completely absorbed into the Germanic feudal system. Churches and monasteries became the property of the men who founded them, not the Church, and civil rulers asserted the right to "invest" clerics with the symbols of office and the grants of land that went with the office. Needless to say, simony—the practice of buying Church offices—became ubiquitous. As a result, the moral standing of the clergy went down hill, with the rule of clerical celibacy routinely ignored.[26]

By the end of the tenth century, the Roman Catholic Church was, to put it bluntly, in a mess. In the eleventh century, the papal throne was occupied by a succession of reforming popes, who sought to restore both moral and proper ecclesiastical order to the Church. While one can only applaud the reform of these abuses, especially the Church's victory over the practice of lay investiture, the Gregorian Reforms—as they came to be

[25]Of course, Rome reaffirmed her traditional prerogatives within the universal Church, but the East had never denied these. What was denied, of course, was the claim to universal jurisdiction.

[26]For an excellent overview see Aristeides Papadakis, *The Christian East and the Rise of the Papacy: The Church 1071-1453 A.D.* (Crestwood, NY: SVS Press, 1994), pp. 17ff. Cited hereafter as *Christian East*. See also Dvornik, *Byzantium*, pp. 128ff.

known—went far beyond fixing the canonical problems created by the Church's absorption into the feudal system.[27]

Ironically, the reforming popes, almost without exception, were not Romans, but Franks (Germans). From the Rhineland they brought not only a desire to end the corruption that had plagued the Church, but a dedication to the Frankish theological program as well.[28]

In 962—in a replay of Charlemagne's coronation in 800—Pope John XII crowned Otto I emperor. Otto promptly declared that all future popes would have to swear loyalty to the German crown before taking office. The result of this was that the papacy was now open to German clerics. Aristeides Papadakis notes:

> Although the German move in 962 was entirely political in character, it was not long before theology entered the picture as well. The seizure of the papacy by German forces actually also marks the gradual revival of German theological influence at the papal court. This is perhaps most obvious with the *Filioque*, or doctrine of the double

[27]"The reformers saw no other remedy than the restoration of the power and influence of the papacy as a means of freeing the Church from the stifling influence of the lay power. The principle was fundamentally good...Unfortunately, these reformers were totally unaware of the peculiar situation of the Eastern churches and they naturally wished to extend everywhere the direct right of intervention of the papacy—even in the East where the churches had enjoyed a good deal of autonomy in running their internal affairs according to their own custom." Dvornik, *Byzantium*, p. 129.

[28]Cf. Dvornik, *Byzantium*, pp. 126-127.

procession. Granted this formula had by then spread throughout northern Europe and had been added to the creed before the tenth century. On the other hand, this had been achieved without official papal approval or authorization. Rome had condemned the extra phrase on more than one occasion; it had even been its primary opponent in the West since Charlemagne's advisors had seen fit to pronounce on its orthodoxy. Be this as it may, after 962 the papacy began to waver on the matter and at the coronation of the German emperor Henry II the formula was introduced into Rome as well (1014). It was a good example of the triumph of German theology south of the Alps after Otto's coronation, although it was not the last. Presently, we will see that many of the agents of the Gregorian reform were of German origin or members of the German episcopate. In fact, the ideology of the reformation will be implemented initially almost entirely by an inner circle of non-Roman northerners, even Rhinelanders.[29]

As part of their reform program, the German popes began to systematically dismantle the theological program of previous popes. By introducing the *Filioque* into the creed at Rome, they deliberately contradicted the decision of the Eighth Council of 879. Indeed, from the eleventh century, this council was dropped from the Roman canonical collections and replaced with the anti-

[29]Papadakis, *Christian East,* p. 29.

Photian council of 869—a council repudiated by John VIII and his immediate successors.[30]

In addition to introducing the *Filioque*, the German popes also began to assert the previously repudiated (Council of 879) claims to universal jurisdiction. Gregory VII's *Dictatus papae* clearly set the tone for the papal program. Among the twenty-seven statements in the *Dictatus*:[31]

> 2. That the Roman pontiff alone is rightly to be called universal.

> 3. That he alone can depose or reinstate bishops.

> 12. That he may depose emperors.

> 19. That he himself may be judged by no one.

> 22. That the Roman Church has never erred, nor ever, by the witness of Scripture, shall err to all eternity.[32]

Although not all of these ideas were new in the eleventh century, the systematic application of these principles was. The result was nothing less than a

---

[30]The council of 869 is still listed as the Eighth Ecumenical Council of the Roman Catholic Church.

[31]Papadakis, *Christian East*, pp. 47ff.

[32]This conveniently ignores the fact that Pope Honorius was condemned by the Sixth Ecumenical Council for supporting heretics and that this council, with the condemnation of Honorius, was affirmed by all popes at their coronation...until the eleventh century!

transformation of the very nature of the papacy.[33] Not only did the new papal theology lead to schism with the East, it transformed the relationship between the pope and the Western bishops, who became little more than vicars of the pope.[34]

By the end of the eleventh century, therefore, the papacy had been taken over by ethnic Germans who imposed the German (Frankish) theological program on the entire Western Church. The Eighth Ecumenical Council, confirmed by John VIII and accepted as authoritative since the ninth century, was repudiated. The *Filioque*, refused by previous popes and condemned by John VIII, was enshrined in the creed in Rome and made dogma. Furthermore, popes began to claim the right to rule over the entire Church—East and West—a claim that had never been accepted by the East and was repudiated by the pope himself in 879.

Thus, in the eleventh century, the Roman Catholic Church ceased to be either Roman or catholic. With the papacy in the hands of German clerics, the unchangeable Nicene Creed was changed, the ancient system of ecclesiastical government was overturned, and the thousand year-old unity of the Church was sundered. This was no longer the Church of Clement, Leo I, Gregory I (the Great), or John VIII. It was a new and different church—a new and different form of Christianity.

[33]Dvornik describes the *Dictatus* as manifesting "a new political ideology." *Byzantium*, p. 137.
[34]Papadakis, *Christian East*, pp. 50-51.

CHAPTER TWO
The Holy Trinity

*Come, all peoples, and let us worship the one
Godhead in three persons, the Son in the Father
with the Holy Spirit. For the Father gave birth
outside time to the Son, co-eternal and
enthroned with Him; and the Holy Spirit is
glorified in the Father together with the Son:
one power, one essence, one Godhead, Whom
we all worship, and to Whom we say: Holy
God, Who hast created all things through the
Son, by the cooperation of the Holy Spirit.
Holy Mighty, through Whom we know the
Father, and through Whom the Holy Spirit
came to dwell within the world. Holy Immortal, Paraclete Spirit, proceeding from the
Father and resting on the Son. Holy Trinity,
Glory to Thee (Vespers of Pentecost Sunday).*

We saw in the last chapter that the introduction of
the *Filioque* into the Creed in Rome was a significant
factor in the dissolution of the unity between the
Church of Rome and the Orthodox Church. Many
people, however, simply cannot understand *why* this
should be so. If both confess faith in the Father, Son,
and Holy Spirit, what possible difference could it make
whether one believes that the Spirit proceeds from the
Father alone or from the Father and the Son together?

It is crucial that we understand that the controversy over the *Filioque* was—and is—not an argument about mere words. Nor was it primarily an argument about who has the authority to define doctrine in the Church—although that certainly played a part. Ultimately, the issue goes to the very nature of the God we claim to worship. Just because the East and West both use the term "Trinity," it does not mean that we mean the same thing. Pelikan sums up the issue well:

> The Filioque was not only illegitimate [from the Eastern viewpoint—C.C.], it was also mistaken. It was based on certain theological premises which the East found to be inadequate or erroneous and which became visible in the course of the debates. Several of these lay in the area of what must be called 'theological method,' for they involved differences over the way trinitarian doctrine was to be arrived at. Beyond such methodological differences lay some ultimate, metaphysical differences in the doctrine of God itself... [1]

To understand the Orthodox view of the Trinity, and, consequently, why the Orthodox reject the *Filioque* so vehemently, we must consider how and why the doctrine was developed in the first place. Thus, a brief historical sketch is in order.

The Philosophical Challenge

Our story begins at the dawn of the fourth Christian century, a century that produced four of the

[1]Pelikan, *Spirit*, pp. 192-193.

brightest lights that the Church has ever seen: St. Athanasius the Great, St. Basil the Great, St. Gregory of Nyssa, and St. Gregory the Theologian (Nazianzen). To these men fell the task of expressing in words the mystery of the Trinity, which is beyond all words and human conceptions.

Christianity was born in Jerusalem. The Church is the true Israel, the fulfillment of the promises made by God to the People of Israel. Nevertheless, this Semitic faith was born into a Hellenistic world — that is, a world that had been shaped by the ideas of Greek philosophy and culture. From the very beginning Christians had to find ways to express their faith in a way that was intelligible to a world shaped by Greek modes of thought.[2]

As Christianity expanded throughout the known world, so too did the need to reflect on the mystery of faith and express it more systematically. Yet, the pervasive nature of Greek thought created problems for those who wanted to remain faithful to the essence of the original Christian message.[3]

---

[2]This is evident in St. John's use of *Logos* or Word in the prologue to his Gospel. For over a century, however, Protestant historians have made a cottage industry out of perpetuating the myth that Judaea was somehow exempt from the influences of Hellenism and that one could differentiate between the purely Semitic strains of Christianity (usually represented by St. Paul) and the corrupted, Hellenistic strains represented by later theologians. Martin Hengel brilliantly explodes this myth in *The 'Hellenization' of Judaea in the First Century after Christ* (Philadelphia: Trinity Press International, 1989).

[3]Cf. González, Vol. 1, pp. 159-160.

The second century was the century of the "Apologists" — those who sought to defend Christianity against the attacks of pagan critics. On the whole, the Apologists took one of two approaches to the problem: they either rejected the claims of Greek philosophy outright or they tried to harmonize pagan thought with Christianity, even going so far as to ascribe to Greek philosophy a preparatory role in the advent of Christ parallel to the role played by Israel.[4]

In the third century the influence of the Apologists gave way to the influence of the great school theologians of Alexandria, Egypt. For centuries, Alexandria had been a center of Hellenistic culture and education. It was here that the great Jewish theologian Philo synthesized Jewish and Greek thought (first century BC), and it was here that the first great school of Christian theology was founded.

Clement of Alexandria and Origen stand astride the third century like giants, towering over other theologians of the day. Unfortunately, they were not always successful in their attempt to balance Christian thought with Greek philosophy.[5] Neither is venerated by the Church as a Saint, and Origen's thought was actually condemned by the Church as heresy in 553.

Origen is of concern to us because in many ways he helped to set the stage for the Trinitarian controversies that would rock the fourth century and lead to the

[4]For a general overview see Johannes Quasten, *Patrology*, Vol. 1, *The Beginnings of Patristic Literature* (Westminster, MD: Christian Classics Inc., 1986), pp. 186-253.

[5]See Quasten, Vol. 2, pp. 1-101.

formal elucidation of the doctrine of the Trinity. Origen taught—in keeping with Greek philosophy—that the world (cosmos) was eternal. This, of course, was in direct contradiction to what had been taught by the Prophets and Apostles, namely that God had created the world out of nothing.[6]

Origen reasoned that if God is immutable (unchangeable) and if He is properly called "Father," then He must have always had a Son. Otherwise, He would have begun to be Father at some point in time, introducing change into the deity. So far, so good. He went on to reason, however, that since God is also called "Creator," then the world must have always existed, otherwise He would have begun to create at some point in time, again introducing change into the changeless deity.

Origen's logic was impeccable. The problem was that it led him to a conclusion that was in direct contradiction with what the Church had always taught. Here we see very clearly the clash between Greek philosophy—with its preconceived notions about the nature of God—and the Christian faith. It fell to St. Athanasius of Alexandria, the man who would become the champion of the Orthodox doctrine of the Trinity, to solve the theological problem created by Origen's philosophical speculations.[7]

---

[6]*I beseech you, my child, to look at the heaven and the earth and see everything that is in them, and recognize that God did not make them out of things that existed* (2 Macc. 7:28, RSV). Cf. Heb. 11:3.

[7]For this section I am greatly indebted to Fr. Georges Florovsky's study, "St. Athanasius' Concept of Creation" in *The*

Athanasius' solution was philosophically daring. He drew a sharp distinction between what God *is* in Himself and what He *does*. God is Father because that is what He is. On the other hand, He created the world in time by His will. He could have created or not created. The world is neither eternal nor necessary. God is Creator only because He wills to create.

This distinction between God's inner life and the way He acts outside Himself (*ad extra*) allows us to reflect about God's being in Himself (θεολογία—theology proper) and His activity (οἰκονομία) separately.[8] Now there is no question that such a distinction was an affront to traditional Greek ways of thought, for it challenged the very notion of the Divine Simplicity. Nevertheless, Athanasius understood that he was talking about the Christian God, not the god of the philosophers—the God Who had created the world out of nothing, the God Who had taken flesh and become man.

This distinction was absolutely crucial for the solution of the controversy that would follow concerning the doctrine of the Trinity.[9] Significantly,

Collected Works of Georges Florovsky, Vol. 4, *Aspects of Church History* (Belmont, MA: Nordland, 1975), pp. 39-62. Cited hereafter as "Creation."

[8]Florovsky, "Creation," pp. 52-53.

[9]"Now, the question arises: Is the distinction between 'Being' and 'Acting' in God, or, in other terms, between the Divine 'Essence' and 'Energy,' a genuine and ontological distinction—*in re ipsa*; or is it merely a mental or logical distinction, as it were, κατ᾽ ἐπίνοιαν, which should not be interpreted objectively, lest the Simplicity of the Divine Being is compromised. There cannot be the

however, this distinction—between God's inner life and His activity (later called energies)—would be denied by Latin speaking theologians from the Middle Ages right down to the present. We will return to this point later. At the moment, let us note that St. Athanasius solved the problem created by Origen by positing a real distinction within God between His being and His activity.

The Arian Controversy

We are now ready to turn our attention to the Trinitarian controversies of the fourth century sparked by an Alexandrian presbyter by the name of Arius. In many respects, Arius brought the same set of philosophical presuppositions to the table as Origen had earlier, the difference being that they ended up with diametrically opposed conclusions. Whereas Origen taught that the world was eternal, Arius taught that the Son and Word of God was created. Neither of them was able (or willing) to make the kind of philosophical distinction between God's being and activity that St. Athanasius had made.

As Origen before him, Arius was concerned to defend a fundamentally Greek philosophical notion of God. If, he reasoned, God has an eternal Son, it would

slightest doubt that for St. Athanasius it was a real and ontological difference. Otherwise his main argument against the Arians would have been invalidated and destroyed." Florovsky, "Creation," pp. 61-62.

destroy the Divine Simplicity, making multiple Gods.[10]
The Word, therefore, must be a created being.[11]

From the very beginning, the Church had
worshipped Christ as God. If Arius was correct,
however, it meant that the Church had been wor-
shipping a creature, which was blasphemy. Not sur-
prisingly, Alexander, the bishop of Alexandria, publicly
condemned Arius. Unfortunately, the controversy did
not end there. Arius had many supporters in
Alexandria and found new supporters in Antioch and
elsewhere. Before long, "Arianism" became a serious
threat to the unity of the Church throughout the world.
It was this threat that prompted the Emperor
Constantine to call for a universal council of the Church
to deal with the problem.

Three hundred and eighteen bishops from around
the world—though mostly from the Middle East, Asia
Minor, and the Mediterranean—gathered in Nicea, a
suburb of Constantinople, in 325 to deal with the Arian
controversy. The Arian case was presented by Eusebius,

[10]González, Vol. 1, pp. 161ff. Pelikan notes Arius' emphasis on
the fact that God is by nature one and alone: "The fundamental
idea in the Arian doctrine of God was 'one and only' [μόνος]...No
understanding of the Logos as divine could be permitted in any
way to compromise this arithmetical oneness of God, who 'alone'
created his 'only' Son. Originally and fundamentally, then, 'God
was alone.'" *The Christian Tradition*, Vol. 1, *The Emergence of the
Catholic Tradition (100-600)* (Chicago: University of Chicago Press,
1971), p. 194. Cited hereafter as *Emergence*.

[11]Arius certainly believed that the Word was superior to all
other created things, being the "firstborn of all creation."
Nevertheless, the Word was to be numbered with creation.

bishop of Nicomedia, and the Orthodox case by Alexander of Alexandria.[12] When the Fathers of the council heard what Arius had actually taught—that the Word of God was a created being—they reacted violently, tearing the speech from Eusebius' hands.[13] They drafted a creedal statement that explicitly repudiated the ideas of Arius. This creed, which would become the basis for what we know today as the Nicene Creed, affirmed that the Son was "begotten, not made," clearly admitting the distinction that St. Athanasius had made earlier between the being and activity of God.

In trying to ensure the defeat of Arianism, the Fathers of the council did something controversial. They introduced a philosophical term into the statement that was designed to stress the unity of the Father and the Son. They said that the Son was "of one substance (*homoousious*) with the Father."[14] The introduction of this term, however, was to prove extremely controversial.

Arianism did not go away with the decision of Nicea. In fact, the controversy got worse, thanks primarily to imperial meddling in Church affairs. This is not the place to go into the sordid history of depositions, exiles, and imperial flip-flops that followed the Council of Nicea. What does concern us, however, is the theological objection to the use of *homoousious* and the way that objection was met by the theology of the

[12]Neither Arius nor Athanasius could vote at the council because they were not bishops.
[13]González, Vol. 1, pp. 162-167.
[14]ὁμοούσιον τῷ Πατρί.

Cappadocian Fathers. It was the theological genius of these men that led to the final vindication of the faith of Nicea and the final form of the Nicene Creed.

The Cappadocian Fathers

Leaving aside the fact that many people switched sides in the controversy depending on which side the emperor happened to be on at the moment, there was a significant number of bishops who were opposed to both Arianism and the use of *homoousious*. Part of the problem was that *homoousious* was both unbiblical—that is, it did not appear in the Scriptures—and it had a good deal of "baggage" because of its use in Greek philosophy.[15] More important, however, were the implications the word had for the relationship between the persons of the Trinity.

The use of *homoousious*—"of the same substance"—clearly affirmed that the Father and the Son were identical in nature. Some bishops feared, however, that in stressing the identity of the persons so strongly, they were in fact eliminating the distinction between the persons. The problem was with the Greek word for person, *prosopon*. Lacking any kind of philosophical connotation, its primary meaning was that of "face" or

[15]It appears in Plotinus (*Enneads* 4:4:28 and 4:7:10), Porphyrius Tyrius (*de Abstinentia* 1:19), and Iamblichus (*de Mysteriis,* 3:21) among others. See "ὁμο-ούσιος, ον" in Henry George Liddell and Robert Scott, *A Greek-English Lexicon* (Oxford: Clarendon Press, 1968).

even "mask."[16] In fact, it was the word used to denote a dramatic role or character in a play.[17] Thus, many bishops feared that the Church had unintentionally fallen into the heresy of Sabellianism.

Sabellius was a Roman presbyter (early third century) who taught that the Father, Son, and Spirit were three "roles" or "modes" that the one God used at different times. Thus, at one point in history God employed the mode of Father. During the Incarnation, He employed the mode or role of the Son. The image is clearly one of the single God putting on different masks at different times. This heresy became known as Sabellianism or Modalism.

You can easily see why many bishops were concerned. *Homoousious* was a philosophical term stressing the fact that the Father and the Son were of the same substance or nature. *Prosopon*, lacking any philosophical import, meant mask or face. The persons of the Trinity were in danger of disappearing into the divine nature.

The problem, however, was not simply that *prosopon* lacked philosophical weight, but that Greek philosophy had never developed a concept of true "personhood."[18] Indeed, the idea of a person as an

[16]Cf. "πρόσωπον" in Liddell and Scott, where "person" is the last definition listed.

[17]The same applies for the Latin word *persona*. Indeed, *dramatis persona* is still used to refer to a theatrical character.

[18]Cf. (Metropolitan) John Zizioulas, *Being as Communion: Studies in Personhood and the Church* (Crestwood, NY: SVS Press, 1985), pp. 27ff. I am greatly indebted to Zizioulas for the material in this section, esp. Chapters One and Two (pp. 27-122).

object of philosophical inquiry is the result of the development of Christian theology.[19] What was needed at that time, therefore, was nothing less than a philosophical revolution.[20]

The revolutionaries were three of the most brilliant men of the age, St. Basil the Great, St. Gregory of Nyssa, and St. Gregory the Theologian—the Cappadocian Fathers. Their solution to the problem was to use a new word for person, a word that had previously been a synonym for substance (*ousia*): *hypostasis*. In doing this, they literally gave "substance" or philosophical weight to the idea of person. For the first time in human history, "person" became a philosophical term.[21]

The result of this was that now the concept of person had the same philosophical weight as the concept of essence or substance, giving balance to the unity of the Trinity and to the distinctiveness of the three divine persons. The persons of the Trinity are not masks or roles that the one, individual God assumes at

[19]"Indeed, our ideas of human personality, of that *personal* quality which makes every human being unique, to be expressed only in terms of itself: this idea of *person* comes to us from Christian theology. The philosophy of antiquity knew only human individuals." Vladimir Lossky, *The Mystical Theology of the Eastern Church* (Crestwood, NY: SVS Press, 1976), p. 53. Cited hereafter as *Mystical Theology*.

[20]Cf. Zizioulas, p. 36.

[21]"The genius of the Fathers made use of the two synonyms to distinguish in God that which is common—ousia, substance or essence—from that which is particular—ὑπόστασις or person." Lossky, *Mystical Theology*, p. 51.

different times, but three distinct *persons* in Whom the one divine nature subsists.

With the personal distinctiveness of each of the persons guaranteed by the use of *hypostasis*, the unity of the Trinity was guaranteed by the common origin or source of the persons: the person of the Father, Who eternally begets His Son and breathes forth His Spirit in an unbroken communion of love. Early on at the Second Ecumenical Council (381), St. Gregory the Theologian stressed this point:

> Now, the name of that which has no beginning is the Father, and of the Beginning the Son, and of that which is with the Beginning, the Holy Spirit, and the three have one Nature—God. And the union is the Father from Whom and to Whom the order of Persons runs its course, not so as to be confounded, but so as to be possessed, without distinction of time, of will, or of power.[22]

The one God, therefore, is not the divine nature, which each of the persons shares in its totality, but the person of the Father. In the creed we do not say "I believe in one God, the divine nature," but "in one God, the Father almighty." As Zizioulas puts it, "What therefore is important in trinitarian theology is that God 'exists' on account of a person, the Father, and not on account of a substance."[23] The Father is thus the

---

[22]Gregory Nazianzus (the Theologian), Oration XLII:15.

[23]Zizioulas, p. 42. Also: "...the Cappadocians' position—characteristic of all the Greek Fathers—lay, as Karl Rahner (*The Trinity*, 1970) observes, in that the final assertion of ontology in

principle (ἀρχὴ), source (πηγαία), and cause (αἴτιον) of the Trinity:

> The Father derives from Himself His being, nor does He derive a single quality from another. Rather He is Himself the beginning and cause of the existence of all things both as to their nature and mode of being.... All then that the Son and the Spirit have is from the Father, even their very being: and unless the Father is, neither the Son nor the Spirit is. And unless the Father possesses a certain attribute, neither the Son nor the Spirit possesses it: and through the Father, that is, because of the Father's existence, the Son and the Spirit exist.[24]

This point is of crucial importance for it underscores the primary concern of the Cappadocian Fathers: to give adequate expression to the God Who had revealed Himself to the Prophets and Apostles. This is not the God of the philosophers—an absolutely simple essence—but the God of Abraham, Isaac, and Jacob.

The Cappadocians did not "invent" the doctrine of the Trinity. They were trying to answer the challenge posed by the succession of heresies that had been plaguing the Church. Sabellianism, Origenism, Arianism—indeed most of the "isms" that have popped up throughout Christian history—all shared a common element: the tendency to subordinate the God of the

God has to be attached not to the unique *ousia* of God but *to the Father*, that is, to a *hypostasis* or person." p.88.

[24]St. John of Damascus, *An Exact Exposition of the Orthodox Faith*, I:8, quoted in Lossky, *Mystical Theology*, pp. 59-60.

Gospels to some preconceived philosophical notion about what God is supposed to be like. The biblical vision of a personal God was inevitably sacrificed for the sake of an absolutely simple and immutable divine essence.

Arianism could never triumph because it made a lie out of the Church's life and worship. She had worshipped Christ from the beginning and knew Him to be God, not a creature.[25] Nevertheless, the Church needed an adequate way to express Her faith in God the Father, God the Son, and God the Holy Spirit. The personalistic theology of the Cappadocian Fathers was the answer to that need. It was the key to reconciling to the Nicene faith those bishops who had opposed the term *homoousion* because of their fear of Sabellianism. This took place at the Second Ecumenical Council, held in Constantinople in 381. This would not have happened, however, without the Cappadocians. The faith of Nicea was accepted within the framework set forth by the Cappadocians, and the final form of the Nicene Creed was established.[26]

It is often stated that the Trinitarian theology of the Cappadocians is simply an alternative to other Trinitarian theologies, such as those of St. Augustine or Thomas Aquinas. Nothing could be further from the truth. The theology of the Second Ecumenical Council *is*

[25]Cf. González, Vol. 1, p. 161.

[26]"Thus, it was this council that definitively proclaimed the doctrine of the Trinity. Its decisions, and the theology reflected in them, were in large measure the result of the work of the Great Cappadocians." González, p. 188.

the theology of the Cappadocian Fathers. When, therefore, Latin speaking theologians inserted the *Filioque* into the Nicene Creed, they not only tampered with the text, they tampered with the very theology of the creed itself. This is why the Orthodox Church reacted so strongly to the addition of the *Filioque*.

The Filioque

It is important to note that the Orthodox did not object to the *Filioque* solely because they opposed the pope's alleged authority to insert it into the creed. While the question of papal authority did play a part in the controversy (primarily because Rome kept asserting it), it was not the main concern. The Orthodox rejected the *Filioque* because it was heretical, not simply because the pope claimed the right to insert it into the Nicene Creed.[27]

At the Second Council of Lyons (1274), considered by the Roman Catholic Church to be the Fourteenth Ecumenical Council,[28] the *Filioque* was defined in this way:

[27]The Roman argument was often the inverse of this: The *Filioque* is true because the pope affirms it. Such a position, however, precludes any real discussion of the issue. If it has been decided *a priori* that the pope cannot be wrong, then there is not much reason to debate the merits of the issue itself. Needless to say, the Orthodox flatly reject this presupposition. See Chapter Four, below.

[28]The council was intended to be a reunion council between the East and West: "It was at this session that the Latin doctrines of purgatory, papal supremacy, and the *Filioque* were solemnly

We profess faithfully and devotedly that the Holy Spirit proceeds eternally from the Father and the Son, not as from two principles, but as from one principle; not by two spirations, but by one single spiration. This the holy Roman Church, mother and mistress of all the faithful, has till now professed, preached and taught; this she firmly holds, preaches, professes and teaches; this is the unchangeable and true belief of the orthodox fathers and doctors, Latin and Greek alike. But because some, on account of ignorance of the said indisputable truth, have fallen into various errors, we, wishing to close the way to such errors, with the approval of the sacred council, condemn and reprove all who presume to deny that the Holy Spirit proceeds eternally from the Father and the Son, or rashly to assert that the holy Spirit proceeds from the Father and the Son as from two principles and not as from one. [29]

Thus, the Roman Catholic Church has officially defined as dogma the belief that the Spirit proceeds from the Father and the Son as from a single source (*ab utroque*).

acknowledged and confessed by the emperor's accredited representatives. To say it once more, no formal public debate on these matters was allowed at the council and none is recorded in the sources. Actually, the addition to the creed was formally declared dogma early in the second session of the council even before the Byzantine delegates had arrived!" Papadakis, *Christian East*, p. 221. Lyons was rejected by the Orthodox. See Appendix C.

[29]Second Council of Lyons (1274), Constitution II:1. The *Filioque* was reaffirmed at the Council of Florence (1483). See also the *Catechism of the Catholic Church*, §246-248.

The first systematic Orthodox refutation of the *Filioque* was written by St. Photios the Great, patriarch of Constantinople during the ninth century.[30] We will consider the main points of his attack.

Photios' primary concern in his *Mystagogy* was to demonstrate the logical absurdity of the *Filioque*. According to the Latin doctrine, the Spirit proceeds from both the Father and the Son. Attributes such as generation and procession, however, must be ascribed to either the divine nature, which is common to the

[30]Remember that it was this Photios who was reconciled to Pope John VIII at the Eighth Ecumenical Council held in 879. At that council the Roman Church *condemned* the addition of the *Filioque* to the creed. St. Photios lavishly praised Pope John and his successor, Pope Hadrian, for their Orthodoxy: "Now this man, my John (and a majority of others who are our fathers), is a courageous mind, a courageously pious man, courageous because he abhors and casts down unrighteousness and every manner of impiety not only with sacred doctrine, but also with secular power. This man (favored amongst the Roman archbishops by his more-than-illustrious and God-serving legates Paul, Eugene and Peter, bishops and priests of God, who were with us in the council of the Catholic Church of God), confirmed and subscribed to the Symbol of the Faith, with wondrous and notable sayings, with sacred tongue and hand. Yes, and after that, the holy Hadrian wrote to us according to the prescription of an ancient custom, sending us the same doctrine, testifying for the same theology, namely, that the Spirit proceeds from the Father." *Mystagogy of the Holy Spirit*, 88, trans. by Joseph Farrell (Brookline, MA: Holy Cross Orthodox Press, 1987), p. 105. As we saw above, however, in the eleventh century the Frankish popes disowned the Eighth Council and inserted the clause into the creed in Rome.

three persons, or to one of the persons.[31] It is inconceivable, however, that an attribute could be applied to two of the persons without applying to the third. Otherwise there would be inequality in the Godhead. This means that the property of "spirating" or "producing" the Spirit must either belong to the divine nature or to *one* person of the Trinity. It cannot belong to two persons, unless one is prepared to admit that the third person is not equal to the first two.

St. Photios created a logical dilemma from which the supporters of the *Filioque* were not able to escape. No matter which way you turn, the Holy Spirit ends up as something less than a fully divine person. If one asserts that generation and spiration are properties of nature, then one must assert them of *all* the divine persons.[32] Thus, the persons would all generate and spirate each other. Furthermore, the Spirit, if He is identical in essence with the Father and the Son, must also produce another person (or produce the Father and the Son):

> If the Son is begotten from the Father and the Spirit proceeds from the Son, by what reason do you not accord the Spirit, Who subsists in the same identical essence, the dignity of another procession from

[31]"According to this line of reasoning, everything not said about the whole, omnipotent, consubstantial and supersubstantial Trinity is said about one of the three persons." *Mystagogy*, 36, p. 76.

[32]Among others, Paulinus of Aquileia, Ratramnus, and Peter Damian asserted that the procession of the Spirit was from the divine nature, not the hypostases. See Pelikan, *Spirit*, p. 195.

Himself at the same time? Otherwise, you degrade Him who is worthy of equal honor.[33]

On the other hand, if procession or spiration are considered to be properties of the person, not of the nature, then how can one possibly explain *two* of the persons sharing the same property? Does the Father *need* the Son to produce the Spirit?

> But the essence is not the cause of the Word; the Father is the personal cause of the person of the Word. But if, as this ungodly doctrine asserts, the Son is also a cause of the Spirit, then the personal feature of the Father is distributed to the Son. Ultimately you are forced to say this, or else to say that the Son completes the person of the Father. But to say that is to argue that the person of the Father is imperfect, wanting completion, and that the Son takes over the Father's role and title. This is the same thing as reducing the awesome mystery of the Trinity to a mere dyad.[34]

We should note at this point that one of the primary reasons given for inserting the *Filioque* into the creed was in order to combat the heresy of Arianism. Most of the barbarian tribes had accepted Arian Christianity.[35] Although they eventually converted to the Catholic faith, Arianism occasionally made comebacks in the West under various guises. Spain was a particular

---

[33]*Mystagogy*, 8, pp. 62-63.
[34]*Mystagogy*, 15, pp. 65.
[35]Alaric the Goth, who sacked Rome in 410, was an Arian.

hotbed of heretical speculation.[36] Theologians such as
Paulinus of Aquileia employed the *Filioque* against
those who argued that Christ's humanity had been
"adopted," thus asserting the full equality of the Son
with the Father.[37]

At first glance, the argument seems sound. If Christ
is fully divine, truly God as is His Father, then the Holy
Spirit must proceed from Him as well as from the
Father. While this may "help" to affirm the full divinity
of the Son, it leaves the Holy Spirit out in the cold. If the
Son needs to produce the Spirit (with the Father) in
order to be equal to the Father, then does the Spirit not
also need to produce a person, in order to be equal to
the Father and the Son? There is simply no way to
assert the *Filioque* without subordinating the Spirit.[38] To
quote St. Photios again:

> Furthermore, if the Son is begotten from the Father,
> and the Spirit (according to this innovation)

[36]Pelikan, *Growth*, p. 52. Indeed, the resurgence of both
Arianism and Nestorianism in the West centuries after these
heresies had been officially condemned in the East constitutes what
Pelikan has called "the 'theological lag' of the West behind the
East." *Spirit*, p. 184. The *Filioque* may have first been used in an
official context at the anti-Arian Council of Toledo in 589. Cf. J.N.D.
Kelly, *Early Christian Creeds* (New York: 1981), pp. 361-362.

[37]Pelikan, *Spirit*, pp. 185-186.

[38]I find it interesting that the "charismatic" or "pentecostal"
movement has had very little success in the Orthodox world while
Protestants and Roman Catholics alike have enthusiastically
embraced it. Could it be that this "rediscovery" of the Spirit in the
West is a reaction to the effects of the subordination of the Spirit in
Western theology?

proceeds from the Father and the Son, then by the same token another person should proceed from the Spirit, and so we should have not three but four persons! And if the fourth procession is possible, then another procession is possible from that, and so on to an infinite number of processions and persons, until at last this doctrine is transformed into a Greek polytheism![39]

The fact is that although the *Filioque* may have been used in the adoptionist controversies, the doctrine was not created to fight Arianism. The *Filioque* had been around in some form since at least the fifth century. Its almost unanimous acceptance by later Latin speaking theologians was due not to its theological necessity (in fighting Arianism) but to the authority of St. Augustine and to the theological method that would become the common currency of Western Christianity:

> The most striking, and ecumenically the most fateful, example of the pervasive authority of Augustine in Latin trinitarian theology was the almost automatic manner in which Western theologians accepted the idea of the Filioque.[40]

In accounts of the *Filioque* controversy, it is almost *de rigueur* to note that that Eastern theologians usually began with the persons of the Trinity and then worked their way to the unity of the nature, while Western theologians usually began with the one nature and

[39]*Mystagogy*, 37, p.77.
[40]Pelikan, *Growth*, p.21.

worked their way to the plurality of divine persons.[41]
Scholarly orthodoxy and ecumenical politeness also
require one to immediately affirm that *both* approaches
are legitimate, so long as neither goes to an extreme in
asserting either tritheism or Sabellianism.[42]

I cannot agree with this. It is not enough merely to
state the obvious. The question is *why* did Eastern and
(later) Western theologians take such different
approaches? These are not complementary approaches
to one and the same mystery, but divergent paths,
destined to arrive at different and irreconcilable visions
of God. If the Orthodox insistence upon starting with
the persons of the Trinity was a reflection of their
concern to maintain a fundamentally biblical view of
God—the God of Abraham, Isaac, and Jacob—the Latin
insistence upon starting with the divine nature reflects
a fundamentally philosophical approach to theology.[43]

[41]Cf. T.R. Martland, "A Study of Cappadocian and
Augustinian Trinitarian Methodology," *Anglican Theological Review*,
47 (1965), p. 256.

[42]This is true of Orthodox scholars as well. Cf. Lossky, *Mystical
Theology*, p. 52 and *Papadakis, Crisis in Byzantium: The Filioque
Controversy in the Patriarchate of Gregory II of Cyprus (1283-1289)*
(Crestwood, NY: 1997), p. 86. Both Lossky and Papadakis,
however, go on to demonstrate why the *Filioque*—a logical
development from the Western approach to the Trinity—is
heretical.

[43]Cf. Meyendorff, *The Byzantine Legacy in the Orthodox Church*
(Crestwood, NY: SVS Press, 1982), pp. 154ff. The same applies to
the Nestorian controversy, where it is often asserted that the
Nestorians started with the two natures and worked back to the
unity of subject in Christ while the Orthodox started with the unity
of the subject and reasoned back to the two natures. Again, the

As with Arius and Origen, defenders of the *Filioque* were unable to conceive of real distinctions within the Godhead because of their emphasis on the Divine Simplicity. Indeed St. Augustine was quite clear about the simplicity of the divine nature: "God is His own Perfection, is 'simple', so that His wisdom and knowledge, His goodness and power, are His own essence, which is without accidents."[44]

Because of this insistence on the Divine Simplicity, Latin theologians rarely distinguished between the eternal (ontological) procession of the Spirit from the Father and His temporal (economic) manifestation from the Son. Advocates of the *Filioque* would quote verses such as John 20:22: *And when He had said this, He breathed on them, and saith unto them, Receive ye the Holy Spirit.* This, they said, was proof that the Spirit proceeded eternally from the Son as well as the Father. Orthodox theologians pointed out, however, that in the same Gospel Christ Himself delineates between the temporal mission of the Spirit and His eternal procession: *But*

question is *why?* And, again, the answer is the same: the Nestorians were positing an essentially philosophical doctrine of Christ whereas the Orthodox were championing a genuinely biblical vision, which emphasized that it was no less than the Son of God Himself who was born, crucified, and rose again for our salvation.

[44]Frederick Copleston, S.J., *A History of Philosophy*, Vol. 2, Pt. 1, *Mediaeval Philosophy: Augustine to Bonaventure* (Garden City, NY: Image Books, 1962), p. 87. This raises several unanswered questions for Augustine's theology. Did this contribute to his doctrine of predestination? If predestination and foreknowledge are one and the same, then God must predestine all that He foreknows.

when the Comforter is come, whom I will send unto you from the Father, even the Spirit of truth, which proceedeth from the Father, He shall testify of Me (John 15:26).

The Orthodox never denied that the Son sent the Spirit into the world or that the Spirit proceeds *through* the Son (in reference to His temporal mission).[45] The Filioquists, however, conflated the temporal mission and the eternal procession of the Spirit.[46]

Similarly, the emphasis placed on the absolute simplicity of divine nature by the advocates of the *Filioque* could only result in depreciation and undervaluing of the persons. To answer this criticism, some Latin speaking theologians,

> attempted to locate the procession 'neither in the ousia, which is common [to all the persons], nor in the person, which is spoken of in itself, but in the relation [between persons].'[47]

Thus, the personal life of the Trinity is reduced to the category of relations. Indeed, it is commonplace even today for Roman Catholic theologians to deny that there is a real (as opposed to a merely semantic) difference between person and nature.[48]

[45]The *Libri Carolini* specifically asserted that the Spirit proceeds from the Son rather than through the Son. Pelikan, *Spirit*, p. 186.

[46]Pelikan, *Spirit*, pp. 193-194.

[47]Pelikan, *Spirit*, p. 195. The reference is to Anselm of Havelberg, *Dialogues in Constantinople with Nicetas of Nicomedia*, 2:10.

[48]See François-Marie Léthel, *Théologie de L'Agonie du Christ* (Paris: Éditions Beauchesne, 1979), p. 83.

Thus, from the time of St. Augustine on, Western theologians adopted a fundamentally philosophical approach to theology, one in which speculation about the divine essence predominated. The *Filioque* is the fruit of this method. Of course, St. Augustine had no intention of being anything other than a faithful son of the Church.[49] In his *Confessions* one is given a vision of a man of true faith and piety. In his *De Trinitate*, however, Augustine the speculative theologian comes to the fore.[50]

In fairness, we should note that not all scholars agree that St. Augustine posits an "essentialist" or "monistic" view of the Trinity. Rowan Williams argues that Augustine's model of the Trinity is not impersonal or unipersonal, but no less relational than that of the Greek Fathers.[51] Catherine Osborne argues that the

[49]Orthodox appraisals of St. Augustine are routinely negative, some needlessly so. I cannot agree with Christos Yannaras' quip that Augustine is "the fount of every distortion and alteration in the Church's truth in the West." *The Freedom of Morality* (Crestwood, NY: SVS Press, 1984), p. 151, n10. For a more balanced view see Fr. Seraphim Rose, *The Place of Blessed Augustine in the Orthodox Church* (Platina, CA: St. Herman of Alaska Brotherhood, 1983).

[50]For an overview of Augustine's mixture of Aristotelian philosophy and Neo-Platonism in the *De Trinitate*—and the contradictions inherent in that mixture—see A. C. Lloyd, "On Augustine's Concept of a Person" in *Augustine: A Collection of Critical Essays*, ed. by R. A. Markus (Garden City, NY: Anchor Books, 1972), pp. 191-205.

[51]"*Sapentia* and the Trinity: Reflections on the *de Trinitate*," *Augustiniana* 40 (1990), pp. 317-332. Williams argues that in the last two books of *De Trinitate* Augustine suggested a relational or

conception of the Spirit as an impersonal bond of love between the Father and the Son is not to be found in Augustine.[52] Nevertheless, what we are dealing with

personalistic model for understanding the Trinity: "The divine essence is not an abstract principle of unity, nor a 'causal' factor over and above the hypostases: to be God at all is to be desirous of and active in giving the divine life (p. 325)." Again: "God is in love with God, and the God whom God loves is the God who loves God: threefold *caritas* with no extraneous conditioning (p. 325)." I must admit that I find Williams' argument somewhat strained. It is interesting, however, that he flatly denies that Augustine taught the procession of the Spirit from the Father and the Son *as from a single source*, noting that for Augustine, the spirit proceeds *principaliter* from the Father (p. 328). Although Williams is concerned to challenge the conventional Eastern view of Augustine, he is forced, however, to admit a major point of difference between Augustine and the Cappadocian Fathers: "Augustine insists in precisely these passages (xxvi.47-xxvii.48) on the absolute simultaneity of the trinitarian relations, in a way which makes it impossible to accept any crude account of the Father's priority, or even any model of the trinity in which the Father as prime 'possessor' of the divine essence distributes it to the others (we have noted that the divine persons do not 'possess' the divine essence, but are what it is) (p. 328)." Thus, even according to Williams, Augustine was unable to conceive of the Father as the unique source and principle of unity in the Trinity.

[52]"The *nexus amoris* in Augustine's Trinity," *Studia Patristica* 18:3, pp. 308-314. Osborne argues that, unlike later Latin writers, Augustine never referred to the Spirit as an impersonal bond of love between the Father and the Son. Indeed, she raises the possibility that later theologians such as Aquinas may have misinterpreted Augustine. In the process, she offers an interesting critique of the idea of the Spirit as the bond of love: "If love is the bond uniting lover to the beloved, such a bond will be formed if God the Father loves God the Son. But if God the Son loves God the Father there will be another bond between lover and beloved in

here is not so much what Augustine actually said as with what those who followed him *thought* he said. In other words, we are dealing primarily with Augustine's legacy, rather than with Augustine himself.[53]

Summary

If this book accomplishes nothing else, I hope that it will lay to rest the oft-repeated opinion that the *Filioque* controversy is simply an argument about words. First of all, it is an illicit addition to the Nicene Creed. As we

which the Son is lover and the Father beloved. It is hard to see how we could define the two bonds as the same. For a bond to exist it is sufficient that there be a lover and a beloved, and there is no requirement that the love be mutual. Thus although the bond idea may look attractive to supporters of the *filioque* in fact it seems in danger of resulting in two spirits (p. 313)."

[53]Augustine's corpus is so large, and was written over such a long period of time, that it is possible to derive multiple interpretations of Augustine on the same subject. It has often been noted that the Reformation was largely a battle of two distinct emphases within the one Augustinian tradition. If one is intent on finding a single culprit, perhaps more attention should be given to Boethius and his role as an arbiter between classical philosophy and theology in the West. Consider the following from Boethius' *De Trinitate*: "But since no relation can be affirmed of one subject alone, inasmuch as a predicate wanting relation is a predicate of substance, the manifoldness of the category of relation, Trinity is secured through the category of relation, and the Unity is maintained through the fact that there is no difference of substance, or operation, or generally of any substantial predicate. So then, the divine substance preserves the Unity, the divine relations bring about the Trinity" (*De Trin.* VI).

have pointed out more than once, Pope John VIII condemned the addition in 879. More importantly, however, it manifests a different vision of the Trinity and a different approach to theology than that of the Cappadocian Fathers, whose theology lay behind the final ratification of the creed in 381.

One final question arises in connection with the *Filioque*. Pope John Paul II, on a couple of occasions, has recited the creed *without* the *Filioque*. Would it satisfy Orthodox objections if the Roman Church agreed to remove the *Filioque* from the Nicene Creed? The answer is no. The Roman Church has officially declared the *Filioque* to be a dogma. It cannot simply be dropped from the creed as if it did not exist. It must be recognized as a heresy and formally repudiated.[54] This issue cannot be swept under the rug. It must be addressed, and its solution requires a true repentance— a true change of mind and heart.

[54]The service for the reception of Roman Catholics into the Orthodox Church requires candidates to specifically renounce the *Filioque*: "Dost thou renounce the false doctrine that, for the expression of the dogma touching the Procession of the Holy Spirit, the declaration of our Saviour Christ Himself: 'who proceedeth from the Father': doth not suffice; and that the addition, of man's invention: 'and from the Son': is required?" Isabel Florence Hapgood, *Service Book of the Holy Orthodox-Catholic Apostolic Church* (Englewood, NJ: Antiochian Orthodox Christian Archdiocese of North America), p. 455.

CHAPTER THREE
Salvation

When we were in this harsh captivity, ruled by invisible and bitter death, the Master of all visible and invisible creation was not ashamed to humble Himself and to take upon Himself our human nature, subject as it was to the passions of shame and desire and condemned by divine judgment; and He became like us in all things except that He was without sin, that is, without ignoble passions. All the penalties imposed by divine judgment upon man for the sin of the first transgression—death, toil, hunger, thirst and the like—He took upon Himself, becoming what we are, so that we might become what He is. The Logos became man, so that man might become Logos. Being rich, He became poor for our sakes, so that through His poverty we might become rich. In His great love for man He became like us, so that though every virtue we might become like Him (St. Mark the Monk).

The Nicene Creed states that the Only-Begotten Son and Word of God became incarnate, suffered, and died "for us men and for our salvation." Both East and West affirm without qualification that God is at work in the

76

world for the salvation of mankind as a whole and of each and every person in particular.[1] There can, therefore, be no more important topic of human concern than salvation itself.

Although the Orthodox and Roman Catholic Churches have a similar sacramental structure, the differences we noted above in regard to the doctrine of the Trinity also manifest themselves in the way Orthodox and Roman Catholics understand the mystery of salvation. For the Orthodox, salvation is summed up by the word *theosis* — or deification.[2] The purpose of human life and the content of man's salvation is to become a *partaker of the divine nature* (2 Peter 2:10), that is, to become like God, sharing fully in His abundant, eternal life. This understanding of salvation is expressed primarily with metaphors and images concerned with health. Sin is viewed as a *disease*, which leads to spiritual death. Christ, the Great Physician, through His Incarnation, death, resurrection, and ascension, heals and restores human nature, enabling us to participate in the divine life of God.

While the concept of *theosis* is not unknown in the West — it is usually expressed as *sanctification* — the Roman Catholic Church has a very different understanding of salvation from that of the Orthodox Church. Without question, the dominant paradigm

---

[1]This is not to suggest that that all men *must* or even *will* be saved. Both the Orthodox and Roman Catholics affirm the freedom of the human will and the fact that some people will indeed choose eternal perdition rather than eternal life.

[2]θέωσις.

used by Roman Catholics to express the mystery of salvation is that of a legal transaction. Sin is viewed as a crime against the divine justice.[3] Christ came to free man from the eternal—though not necessarily the temporal—punishment due for man's offence against God. The Roman doctrines of merit, purgatory, and indulgences—all unknown in the Orthodox world—are tied to this forensic or legal understanding of salvation.[4]

In this chapter I shall argue that this difference of approaches is more than simply a preference for one metaphor over another, but is rooted in the very different ways Orthodox and Roman Catholics approach theology. The Roman Catholic refusal to accept the distinction between essence and energies as well as the distinction between nature and person leads Roman Catholics to understand salvation in a fundamentally external, legalistic way.

[3]"Sin is nothing else than a morally bad act (St. Thomas, *De malo*, 8:3), an act not in accord with reason informed by the Divine law." A.C. O'Neil, "Sin" in *The Catholic Encyclopedia* (Encyclopedia Press, Inc., 1913).

[4]It is certainly true that since Vatican II the Roman Church has employed non-forensic metaphors with greater frequency. For example, the Sacrament of Penance is now called Reconciliation. Furthermore, the New Roman *Catechism* contains many references to Eastern Fathers and often employs terminology associated with the Orthodox patristic tradition. However, a shift in vocabulary, which many see simply as a concession to liberalism, does not necessarily imply a change in understanding. The legalistic framework for understanding salvation, as expressed by the Councils of Florence and Trent, is still binding and forms the true dogmatic basis for Roman soteriology.

Metaphors

I cannot stress strongly enough that, traditionally, Roman Catholic theologians have taken this legalistic imagery as not merely a partial, descriptive metaphor, but as expressing the very nature of sin and man's salvation. For this reason, we need to briefly examine the use of metaphorical language and its limitations.

Jaroslav Pelikan notes that the creed does not attempt to explain the mechanics of salvation.[5] Thus, many different theories about salvation have arisen during the course of Christian history. This in itself is not a bad thing. Salvation is a multifaceted phenomenon that can be viewed from many different perspectives and expressed in many different ways. Indeed, we find various images and metaphors for salvation in the Scriptures.

The holy Prophets and Apostles described the mystery of salvation as the forgiveness of transgressions, as the forgiveness of a financial debt, as a ransom, as the finding of a lost article, as healing, as a return to paradise, etc. They did so for two reasons. First, as we noted above, the mystery of salvation is multifaceted. Thus, many different metaphors are needed to capture different aspects and nuances.

Just as important, however, is the fact that not all persons are at the same spiritual level. Some metaphors are better suited to certain stages of the spiritual life than others. St. Paul wrote to the Corinthians that he was teaching them in accordance with their spiritual

[5]*Emergence*, p. 141.

maturity: *I have fed you with milk, and not with meat: for hitherto ye were not able to bear it, neither yet now are ye able* (1 Cor. 3:2). The Fathers of the Church also noted that Christians live at different levels of maturity:

> The fear of hell trains beginners to flee from evil; the desire for the reward of good things gives to the advanced the eagerness for the practice of virtues. But the mystery of love removes the mind from all created things, causing it to be blind to all that is less than God. Only those who have become blind to all that is less than God does the Lord instruct by showing them more divine things.[6]

Notice that St. Maximus says that different things motivate men at different stages in their spiritual growth. Initially we are motivated by the fear of punishment. As Solomon wrote, *The fear of the LORD is the beginning of wisdom* (Prov 9:10). As we progress, we work toward the rewards that God has promised those who obey Him. *Eye hath not seen, nor ear heard, neither have entered into the heart of man, the things which God hath prepared for them that love Him* (1 Cor. 2:9). Those who achieve perfection, however, live neither out of fear of punishment nor out of the desire for reward, but for the sake of the love of God, which is their only goal. St. John wrote that *perfect love casteth out fear* (1 John 4:18). Thus, we can understand the statement of St. Anthony

---

[6]St. Maximus the Confessor, Chapters on Knowledge 2:9, from *Maximus Confessor: Selected Writings*, trans. by George Berthold (New York: Paulist Press, 1985), p. 149.

the Great: "I no longer fear God, but I love Him. For love casts out fear."[7]

Just as there is a hierarchy of motivations in the spiritual life (fear, desire for reward, love), so too there is a hierarchy of metaphors that are appropriate to these different stages. Some metaphors are particularly suited to those at the beginning of the spiritual life. They are simple, easy to understand, and provide motivation for beginners to continue on the path of salvation. These metaphors, however, are not meant to be taken as *explanations* of the mystery of salvation.

Perhaps the best example of this is the metaphor of Christ as a ransom. Our Lord said that the Son of Man came to give His life *a ransom for many* (Mt. 20:28).[8] This is a very simple image that anyone can understand. Our Lord not only pays for the release of those who were held in captivity, He is Himself the ransom.

However, when we start to push the metaphor and begin to ask *how* it works, we run into problems. To whom was the ransom paid? Origen suggested that the ransom was paid to the devil, but this was not a very satisfactory answer.[9] St. Gregory the Theologian summed up the problem in this way:

> Now we are to examine another fact and dogma, neglected by most people, but in my judgment well worth inquiring into. To whom was that Blood offered that was shed for us, and why was It shed? I

[7]*The Sayings of the Desert Fathers*, trans. by Benedicta Ward (Kalamazoo, MI: Cistercian Publications, 1975), p. 8.
[8]St. Paul also refers to Christ as a ransom. Cf. 1 Tim. 2:6.
[9]Cf. Pelikan, *Emergence*, p. 148.

mean the precious and famous Blood of our God and High Priest and Sacrifice. We were detained in bondage by the Evil One, sold under sin, and receiving pleasure in exchange for wickedness. Now, since a ransom belongs only to Him who holds in bondage, I ask to whom was this offered, and for what cause? If to the Evil One, fie upon the outrage! If the robber receives ransom, not only from God, but a ransom which consists of God Himself, and has such an illustrious payment for his tyranny, a payment for whose sake it would have been right for him to have left us alone altogether. But if to the Father, I ask first, how? For it was not by Him that we were being oppressed; and next, On what principle did the Blood of His Only-Begotten Son delight the Father, Who would not receive even Isaac, when he was being offered by his Father, but changed the sacrifice, putting a ram in the place of the human victim? Is it not evident that the Father accepts Him, but neither asked for Him nor demanded Him; but on account of the Incarnation, and because Humanity must be sanctified by the Humanity of God, that He might deliver us Himself, and overcome the tyrant, and draw us to Himself by the mediation of His Son, Who also arranged this to the honour of the Father, Whom it is manifest that He obeys in all things?[10]

St. Gregory's conclusion is that the ransom is required by the reality of sin and death, that is by the predicament in which man had placed himself. God the Father had no need of a ransom, and the devil, who had

[10]*Oration* 45:22.

enslaved man by deceit, certainly did not deserve it. The reality of sin and death required that humanity be redeemed by the humanity of God. Elsewhere St. Gregory wrote, "We needed an incarnate God, a God put to death that we might live."[11]

Clearly, therefore, the ransom metaphor does not go very far in explaining how we are saved. Let us take another example. Our Lord often likened our salvation to the finding of a lost article, such as a sheep or coin. This is a wonderful image of God searching for those who have gone astray. How humbling and comforting it is to know that God will leave the ninety-nine in order to search for the one who is lost.[12] This image, however, can only be taken so far. For one thing, the lost article is entirely passive. Neither the coin nor the sheep plays any role in its salvation. The metaphor gives us a beautiful picture of how God longs for the salvation of all, but it says nothing about *our* role in the plan of salvation.

Now let us briefly turn our attention to the metaphors preferred by the Orthodox and Roman Catholic Churches. The legalistic imagery most often employed by Roman Catholics says nothing about the inner nature of man or his salvation. To be sure, they deal with the *moral status* of man before God—either guilty and deserving of punishment or declared righteous—but not with man's inner spiritual state. The secular legal system—this is the source of the

[11]*Oration* 45:28.
[12]Cf. Mat. 18:12-14.

83

metaphor—does not care about the inner state of one accused of a crime, but about his guilt or innocence and whether or not he has paid his debt to society. Forensic imagery is, therefore, fundamentally *external*.

On the other hand, the medical imagery preferred by the Orthodox Church emphasizes the inner nature of man and the state of his spiritual well being. A patient who has cancer would benefit little from being declared well by his doctor if he were in fact still sick. Because the medical imagery deals with the spiritual health of man rather than with his moral standing, it allows us to go deeper into the mystery of salvation than the other images we have discussed.

This is not to suggest that there is anything wrong with using legal imagery in talking about salvation. Legal metaphors, like the ransom and lost article metaphors, are biblical and have their place.[13] The problem arises, however, when one takes an illustrative metaphor for an *explanation*. This is exactly what has happened with Roman Catholic theology.

Uncreated Grace

St. Athanasius' statement that "God became man that man might become divine" sums up very well the Orthodox view of salvation. Orthodoxy is not so much

---

[13]Occasionally Orthodox authors, in reacting to what has been called the "Western Captivity" of Orthodox theology during the eighteenth and nineteenth centuries, will deny the appropriateness of the forensic metaphors altogether. This, however, is a great overreaction.

concerned with how God views man—as guilty or righteous—but with whether or not man is in fact becoming like God. Archimandrite George, abbot of the Monastery of St. Gregory on Mt. Athos, writes, "A God who does not deify man; such a God can have no interest for us, whether He exists or not."[14]

The Orthodox understanding of *theosis* is grounded in doctrine and confirmed by the living experience of those who have undergone *theosis* themselves and have become *partakers of the divine nature* (2 Peter 1:4). This fact was brought to the forefront during a fourteenth-century controversy between advocates of Western theology and the Orthodox Fathers of Mt. Athos.

The so-called Palamite controversy clearly illustrates the differences between the Orthodox and Roman Catholic approaches to salvation. Monks on Mt. Athos had practiced a method of prayer called *hesychasm*[15] for centuries. This method was centered on the constant repetition of the Jesus Prayer.[16] Those who had advanced far along the path of spiritual purification and illumination were said both to see and be seen within the divine light that shone around Christ on the Mount of Transfiguration. Thus, they experienced in this life a foretaste of the future deification of man in the Kingdom of Heaven.

---

[14]Archimandrite George Capsanis, *The Eros of Repentance*, trans. by Fr. Alexander Golitzen (Newbury, MA: Praxis Institute Press), p. 24.

[15]Lit. "stillness"

[16]There are several variations, but the most common form is "Lord Jesus Christ, Son of God, have mercy on me, the sinner."

The Orthodox fathers of Mt. Athos understood this light to be nothing else than the uncreated divine grace—or energy—of God. These monks, like the Apostles with Christ on Mt. Tabor, had been granted a direct, unmediated experience of God's deifying presence.

Two men, however, denied this. Barlaam the Calabrian and Akyndinos could not accept this vision of divine light and argued that what the monks saw was not the divine energy, but a created phenomenon. These men were challenged by St. Gregory Palamas, who has since become hailed in the Orthodox world as one of the great defenders of Orthodoxy against heresy.[17]

The controversy was not about methods of prayer but about the nature and reality of man's salvation.[18] The Orthodox claimed to have a direct, unmediated participation in the life of God (the uncreated energies of God), while Barlaam and Akyndinos denied this. According to them—and according to Roman Catholic

[17]St. Gregory Palamas, Archbishop of Thessalonica, is commemorated as a champion of Orthodoxy on the second Sunday of Great Lent.

[18]For details of the controversy see John Meyendorff, *A Study of Gregory Palamas*, trans. by George Lawrence (Crestwood, NY: SVS Press, 1974) and Vladimir Lossky, *The Vision of God*, trans. by Asheleigh Moorhouse (Crestwood, NY: SVS Press, 1983), pp. 153ff. The literature on the controversy is abundant, although Orthodox and Roman Catholic interpretations differ greatly. See also M. Jugie, "Palamas" and "Palamite (Controverse)" in the *Dictionnaire de Théologie Catholique*.

theology—grace is created. Man can be united with God only through created intermediaries.

We saw in the previous chapter that two philosophical distinctions were necessary in order to properly express—insofar as this is humanly possible—the mystery of the Trinity. The first of these distinctions is that between God's being and His activity, that is between His innermost essence, which is utterly unknowable and unapproachable, and His energies, through which He creates, sustains, and deifies man. The second distinction is between person and nature. The Orthodox theology of salvation—and the theology of St. Gregory Palamas[19]—is based upon these two distinctions.

The problem is this: If God is uncreated, ultimately unknowable and imparticipable, how can man become a *partaker of the divine nature*? If we were to become united with the indivisible divine nature, would we not *become* that nature, becoming equal to God? Is this not blasphemy? On the other hand, can we become absorbed into one of the persons of the Trinity? Can we as persons become members of the Trinity? If man cannot become one with the unapproachable nature of

---

[19]St. Gregory's theology is often called "Palamism." This appellation, however, is highly misleading. Orthodoxy knows no "isms"—such as Augustinianism or Thomism—or schools of theology. St. Gregory's theology is simply Orthodox theology. The term "Palamism" was coined by Roman Catholic theologians who believe that his theology is *not* identical with that of the Fathers of the first few centuries. In fact, it is the theology of the Roman Catholics that has changed. St. Gregory is in perfect continuity with the early Fathers of the Church.

God, and cannot be absorbed into one of the persons or become an additional member of the Trinity, then if man is to have a *real* participation in the life of God, it must be through God's uncreated energies:

> There are three realities in God, namely, substance, energy and a Trinity of divine hypostases. Since it has been shown above that those deemed worthy of union with God so as to become one spirit with Him (even as the great Paul said, "He who clings to the Lord is one spirit with Him.") are not united to God in substance, and since all theologians bear witness in their statements to the fact that God is imparticipable in substance and the hypostatic union happens to be predicated of the Word and God-man alone, it follows that those deemed worthy of union with God are united to God in energy and that the spirit whereby he who clings to God is one with God is called and indeed is the uncreated energy of the Spirit and not the substance of God, even though Barlaam and Akindynos may disagree. For God foretold through the prophet not "My Spirit," but rather, "Of My Spirit I will pour out upon those who believe."[20]

[20]St. Gregory Palamas, *The One Hundred and Fifty Chapters*, §75, trans. by Robert E. Sinkewicz (Toronto: Pontifical Institute of Medieval Studies, 1988), p. 171. Vladimir Lossky explains the issue in this way: "We are unable, therefore, to participate in either the essence or the hypostases of the Holy Trinity. Nevertheless, the divine promise cannot be an illusion: we are called to participate in the divine nature. We are therefore compelled to recognize in God an ineffable distinction, other than that between His essence and His persons, according to which He is, under different aspects, both totally inaccessible and at the same time accessible. This

In a nutshell, the issue is this: is the grace by which man is saved a created phenomenon or the uncreated energy of God? If the former, then how can man become a *partaker of the divine nature*? Salvation can thus be conceived only in terms of an external, moral similitude to God. Christianity then becomes reduced to a system of ethics. In the final analysis, this is what happened in Western Christianity.

Person and Nature

The distinction between God's essence and energies guarantees the *reality* of man's deification. The distinction between person and nature helps us to understand *how* the salvation of mankind is accomplished. Man was created in the image of God. This means that each person shares a common human nature with all other men. At the same time, however, each person is unique and unrepeatable. Moreover, each and every person sums up the one human nature within himself. Every person is, therefore, "catholic" — a unique individual summation of the whole of human nature.

The devil tempted Eve by promising that the fruit of the earth (the Tree of the Knowledge of Good and

distinction is that between the essence of God, or His nature, properly so-called, which is inaccessible, unknowable and incommunicable; and the energies or divine operations, forces proper to and inseparable from God's essence, in which He goes forth from Himself, manifests, communicates, and gives Himself." *Mystical Theology*, p. 70.

Evil) would deify her. Adam and Eve's attempt to become like God—apart from and in direct contradiction of the command of God—is the fall of man. Archimandrite George explains it in this way:

> We know that Adam and Eve were misled by the devil and desired to become gods, not in co-operation with God, though, not with humbleness, obedience and love, but relying on their own powers, their own will, egoistically and autonomously. That is to say, the essence of the fall is egotism. By adopting egotism and self-sufficiency, they separated themselves from God and instead of attaining deification, they attained exactly the opposite: spiritual death.[21]

Because human nature is one, the sin of Adam and Eve has affected *all* of humanity. Human nature has become corrupt, and every person born inherits a corrupt nature, enslaved to the passions and to death. This is why the sin of Adam and Eve is often called the Ancestral Sin. It is important to note here, that what we have inherited from Adam and Eve are the *consequences* of their sin—the enslavement to sin and death—not the *guilt* for their sin.

The eternal Son and Word of God—the Second Person of the Trinity—became man so that human nature might be restored and mankind attain the deification for which it was originally created. In becoming man, Christ assumed human nature in its

[21]*The Deification as the Purpose of Man's Life* (Mt. Athos, Greece: Holy Monastery of St. Gregorios, 1997), p. 17.

entirety, taking a human body and soul with all of its natural faculties. Thus, the Word of God lived a truly human life, but in a divine way. Christ's human will was united inseparably to His divine will. Living in complete obedience to the Father as a *man,* Christ restored human nature and its corrupted will.

This is why St. Paul calls Christ the last Adam.[22] He is the root of a new humanity, a humanity freed from the corruption of sin and death.[23] To become a Christian, therefore, is to *put on Christ* (Gal. 3:27), to become a member of His Body (1 Cor. 6:15).

It was not sufficient, however, for Christ to merely assume human nature. Mankind was enslaved to death and to the devil. To heal humanity, Christ had to meet mankind where it was and assume not only human nature, but all of the consequences of the fall. Thus, St. Paul insists that Christ was not only obedient to the Father, but *obedient unto death, even the death of the cross* (Phil 2:8). Christ, the immortal Son of God, died a human death and descended into Hades, that He might destroy the power of death. This is summed up beautifully in the eucharistic canon of St. Basil the Great:

> He gave Himself as a ransom to death, in which we were held captive, sold under sin.[24] Descending through the Cross into Hades — that He might fill all

[22]Cf. 1 Cor. 15:45ff.

[23]In the second century, St. Irenaeus of Lyons spoke of Christ as "recapitulating" human nature in Himself.

[24]Notice that the ransom is paid to death, i.e. the reality of man's enslavement to corruption.

things with Himself — He loosed the pangs of death. He arose on the third day, having made for all flesh a path to the resurrection from the dead, since it was not possible for the Author of Life to be a victim of corruption (Liturgy of St. Basil).

After His resurrection, Christ ascended to His Father, placing the human nature that He had assumed and healed at the right hand of the throne of glory. In Christ, therefore, human nature has not only been healed, but deified — united eternally with God in Heaven. [25]

Because of the death, resurrection, and ascension of Christ, humanity has been definitively and irrevocably *saved*. Because human nature is one, and because Christ has healed and deified that one nature, *all* men will rise from the dead and live eternally.[26] However, we know from the Divine Scriptures, that while all will arise, not all will enjoy the resurrection as a state of blessedness. St. Nicholas Cabasilas wrote:

> The resurrection is the restoration of our human nature. Such things God gives freely, for just as He forms us without us willing it, so He forms us anew though we contributed nothing to it. On the other hand, the Kingdom and vision of God and union with Christ are privileges which depend on willingness…. One need not therefore marvel that while all will live in immortality, it is not all who will live in blessedness. All equally enjoy God's providence for our nature, but it is only those who

[25]Cf. Eph. 2:5-6.
[26]Cf. 1 Cor. 15:20-22.

are devout towards God who enjoy the gifts which adorn their willingness. This is the reason: God indeed wills all good things for all men and imparts to all alike of all His own gifts, both those which benefit the will and those which restore our nature. On our part we all receive the gifts of God which pertain to nature even though we do not desire them, since we cannot escape them.... As for the things which depend on human willingness, such as choosing that which is good, the forgiveness of sins, uprightness of character, purity of soul, love of God—their reward is final blessedness. These things we have the power to accept or to shun. Therefore those who are willing are able to enjoy them, but as for the unwilling, how would it be possible? It is impossible for the unwilling to wish for them or to be compelled to be willing.[27]

Notice that there is a clear distinction here between person and nature. Christ has restored human nature. Yet, we remain free persons. Christ's resurrection causes all of mankind to rise from the dead, but Christ cannot make us love Him. Love must be the free response of the human heart. For those who love Him, the resurrection will be unto eternal blessedness. For those who hate Him, His appearing will be eternal death.

Notice also that St. Nicholas stated that God bestows His mercy equally upon all. He no doubt had in mind the saying of Christ: *for He maketh His sun to rise*

[27]*The Life in Christ*, trans. by Carmino J. deCatanzaro (Crestwood, NY: SVS Press, 1974), pp. 81-83.

on the evil and on the good, and sendeth rain on the just and on the unjust (Mat. 5:45). This is a very important point for understanding the difference between the Orthodox and Roman Catholic approaches to salvation.

According to St. John, *God is love* (1 Jn. 4:8). We also know from the Scriptures that God does not change.[28] Therefore, God loves both the just and the unjust equally. God does not get angry. God does not get offended. These images from the Scriptures are *anthropomorphisms*. They are human characteristics that are attributed to God for a specific didactic purpose, much in the same way we speak of the hand of God or the heart of God. It is inconceivable, however, that human actions should cause God to change — to be offended or be angry.

The difference between the blessed and the damned, therefore, is not in how God treats them, but in how they each experience the presence and love of God. The blessed respond to God in love and experience His love and providential care precisely as that. The unrighteous, however, do not respond to God's love and therefore experience it as wrath and judgement. The objective reality is one and the same — God is love — but the subjective apprehension of that reality determines the state of one's blessedness or damnation. St. Maximus the Confessor wrote:

> God is the sun of justice, as it is written, who shines rays of goodness on simply everyone. The soul develops according to its free will into either wax

[28]Cf. Heb. 13:8.

because of its love for God or into mud because of its love of matter. Thus just as by nature the mud is dried out by the sun and wax is automatically softened, so also every soul which loves matter and the world and has fixed its mind far from God is hardened as mud according to its free will and by itself advances to its perdition, as did Pharaoh. However, every soul which loves God is softened as wax, and receiving divine impressions and characters it becomes 'the dwelling place of God in the Spirit.'[29]

Even the fire of hell is, according to the Fathers of the Church, the love of God, which the damned experience in a negative way.[30] *For our God is a consuming fire* (Heb. 12:29). For the righteous the love of God is a purifying, illumining, and deifying fire.[31] For the unrighteous it is a burning fire.

In order to participate in the life of God—or rather to experience God as a blessing and not a curse—our hearts and souls must be purified. Within the Church this is accomplished through partaking of the holy

---

[29]Chapters on Knowledge 1:12, pp. 130-131.

[30]Cf. Rom 12:20: *Therefore if thine enemy hunger, feed him; if he thirst, give him drink: for in so doing thou shalt heap coals of fire on his head.*

[31]The Fathers often employ the image of heating an iron in a fire as a metaphor for deification. As the iron gets hot it begins to glow and take on the properties of the fire, yet it remains iron. In the same way, man becomes deified by the divine, uncreated grace, taking on the characteristics of God, while remaining human. The iron is not changed into fire, nor is man changed into God, but man participates in the life of God, as the iron participates in the properties of fire.

Mysteries (Sacraments) and ascetical effort. Here the medical imagery used by the Church becomes extremely helpful. If we think of sin as a disease, that which keeps our heart and soul from functioning normally, that is, from turning toward and resting in God, then we can think of the Mysteries as medical procedures and medicines. St. Ignatius of Antioch referred to the Eucharist as the "medicine of immortality." Similarly, we can think of the sacrament of confession as a form of surgery, where festering cancers of sin are removed. The object is the healing of the human person and the restoration of saving communion with God.

It would be pointless, however, for someone with lung cancer to undergo chemotherapy or even radical surgery if he were not willing to give up smoking, the cause of his cancer. Good health requires not only that diseases be cured, but that we eat healthily, exercise, and avoid those things that cause disease. This is where asceticism comes in. The Church, which is often described in Orthodox literature as a spiritual hospital, has given us the methods of prayer, fasting, almsgiving, etc. as a means of helping to restore our spiritual health. These are not attempts to earn merit or reward before God, but rather therapeutic exercises.

When a confessor prescribes a penance for someone, it is not a punishment—such a notion is utterly obnoxious to the Orthodox spirit. It is analogous to a cardiologist prescribing exercise for one of his patients. It is not a matter of making up for sins or undergoing due punishment, but of doing things to prepare the body (in this case, the spiritual body) for the reception of the medicines (the Eucharist) and training it to fight off disease (sin) in the future. This is why, in the prayers before confession, the priest stresses to the penitent the therapeutic nature of what is about to happen: "Take care, therefore, to tell me all things that thou hast done, lest having come to the physician thou depart unhealed."[32]

This understanding of salvation is based upon the living experience of those who have been purified in heart and have had a foretaste of the experience of the uncreated glory of God. The Orthodox speak about salvation, therefore, from the conviction of experience. This explains why the Orthodox react so strongly against the Roman Catholic understanding of salvation.

Salvation According to Rome

At the heart of the Roman Catholic understanding of salvation is the notion of "satisfaction." According to

[32]I am not using "therapeutic" in the contemporary, secular sense as a means of helping people "cope" with life. Orthodoxy is not interested in helping man cope or in his moral improvement, but in his deification. Fr. Alexander Schmemann offers an excellent critique of modern religion as (secular) therapy in *For the Life of the World: Sacraments and Orthodoxy* (Crestwood, NY: SVS Press, 1988). For an understanding of the genuinely Orthodox approach to the spiritual life as therapy, I highly recommend Metropolitan Hierotheos (Vlachos), *The Illness and Cure of the Soul in the Orthodox Tradition*, trans. by Effie Mavromichali (Levadia, Greece: Birth of the Theotokos Monastery, 1993, and *Orthodox Psychotherapy: The Science of the Fathers*, trans, by Esther Williams (Levadia, Greece: Birth of the Theotokos Monastery).

this theory, God's eternal justice and majesty is offended by the sin of man. As with any crime, justice requires that every sin be punished. This understanding is rooted not so much in the Scriptures, but in Roman law. Pelikan explains:

> Yet the development of the doctrine of the death of Christ was to be shaped by another term, "satisfaction," which Tertullian seems to have introduced into Christian language but which was to find its normative exposition only in the Middle Ages. Tertullian's doctrine of "satisfaction" may have come from Roman private law, where it referred to the amends one made to another for failing to discharge an obligation, or from Roman public law, which enabled the term to be interpreted as a form of punishment.[33]

According to Roman theology, sin entails both eternal and temporal punishment. By His death on the Cross, Christ satisfied God's anger toward our sin, making possible the justification of man before God. However, even after being justified, the temporal punishment due to sin remains. This too must be satisfied:

> The second kind of satisfaction, that namely by which temporal punishment is removed, consists in this, that the penitent after his justification gradually cancels the temporal punishments due to his sins, either *ex opere operato*, by conscientiously performing the penance imposed on him by his

[33]Pelikan, *Emergence*, p. 147.

confessor, or *ex opere operantis*, by self-imposed penances (such as prayer, fasting, almsgiving, etc.) and by bearing patiently the sufferings and trials sent by God; if he neglects this, he will have to give full satisfaction (*satispassio*) in the pains of purgatory (cf. Council of Trent, Sess. XIV, can. xiii, in Denzinger, n. 923).[34]

Notice here that penance is specifically considered to be for the satisfaction of punishment. A man who has been justified by Christ but has not made satisfaction for the temporal punishment due because of his sin goes to purgatory, which is a place of temporal punishment.[35] There, he works off the debt he still owes to God.

A man's period in purgatory may be shortened, however, if the merits of others can be applied to his account. Thus the living may voluntarily assume works of penance or charity in order to win merit for departed loved ones suffering in purgatory.[36] Moreover, the

[34]J. Pohle, "Merit" in the *Catholic Encyclopedia.*

[35]"Purgatory (Lat., 'purgare', to make clean, to purify) in accordance with Catholic teaching is a place or condition of temporal punishment for those who, departing this life in God's grace, are, not entirely free from venial faults, or have not fully paid the satisfaction due to their transgressions." Edward J. Hanna "Purgatory" in the *Catholic Encyclopedia.*

[36]"The possibility of this transfer rests on the fact that the residual punishments for sin are in the nature of a debt, which may be legitimately paid to the creditor and thereby cancelled not only by the debtor himself but also by a friend of the debtor. This consideration is important for the proper understanding of the usefulness of suffrages for the souls in purgatory (cf. Council of

excess merits of the saints are stored up in a treasury and may be applied under certain circumstances to the account of a soul in purgatory. This is known as an indulgence.[37] While the Roman Church no longer *sells* indulgences, as it did in the Renaissance period leading up to the Reformation, the notion of indulgences remains an important aspect of Roman theology.

The Orthodox Church clearly teaches that prayers for the dead are efficacious. When a man dies, he undergoes an initial period of trial, where the demons both accuse him of his past sins and tempt him with the passions that have dominated his life.[38] Thus, prayers are offered for the departed in this time of trial. There is no notion, however of "making up" for past sins or of repaying some debt. God is not in need of reparation and takes no pleasure in the punishment of men. What

Trent, Sess. XXV, *Decret. de purgat.*, in Denzinger, n. 983)." Pohle, "Merit" in the *Catholic Encyclopedia*.

[37]"An indulgence is the extra-sacramental remission of the temporal punishment due, in God's justice, to sin that has been forgiven, which remission is granted by the Church in the exercise of the power of the keys, through the application of the superabundant merits of Christ and of the saints, and for some just and reasonable motive." W.H. Kent, "Indulgences" in the *Catholic Encyclopedia*.

[38]This time of trial is expressed by the metaphor of the soul going through tollhouses. For the best summation of what happens to the soul after death, see Metropolitan Hierotheos [Vlachos], *Life after Death*, Tr. by Esther Williams (Levadia, Greece: Birth of the Theotokos Monastery, 1996). Christ underwent no such trial for, as He said, ...*for the prince of this world cometh, and hath nothing in me* (John 14:30). Similarly, those who have been purified of the passions in this life have no reason to fear such a trial.

is in question is the purity of the soul and its ability to participate in the life of God.

The idea that the soul must undergo temporal punishment is objectionable from several standpoints.[39] First of all, if Christ has died for the forgiveness of sins, then what punishment could possibly remain? Was His sacrifice not sufficient to remit *all* punishment, not just the eternal?[40] Second, the very idea of a temporal, purgatorial fire is unknown to Orthodoxy. The only fire spoken of in the Scriptures is the fire of Gehenna — the permanent abode of the unrighteous *after* the universal resurrection and final judgement. Moreover, Orthodoxy teaches that this fire is not temporal, but is, in fact, the love of God, which the unrighteous experience in a negative way. It is the same fire or light that the Saints experience as the blessedness of deification.

The Roman understanding of sin as the transgression of a law, the doctrines of merit, purgatory, and indulgences are all intertwined in a

---

[39]Purgatory was a major topic of discussion at the Council of Florence (1439-1439). St. Mark of Ephesus defended the Orthodox position against the Roman Catholic doctrine of purgatory. See Ivan N. Ostroumoff, *The History of the Council of Florence,* trans. by Basil Popoff (Boston: Holy Transfiguration Monastery, 1971). Also Met. Hierotheos (Vlachos), *Life After Death,* pp. 147ff.

[40]If one were to grant the idea of sin as a transgression of the law that requires satisfaction, then the Orthodox could agree with traditional Protestant critiques of purgatory. However, Orthodoxy rejects the legalistic framework within which both the Roman Catholic and Protestant soteriologies are located.

single system, each one logically leading to the other.[41] While this system may make perfect sense to anyone raised within the Roman system—or indeed anyone raised within Western Christianity, Protestant or Roman Catholic—it is bewildering to the Orthodox mind. It is a classic example of what happens when theology is based not upon experience, but upon speculation and logical deduction.

Central to the Roman understanding of salvation is the denial of the distinction between God's essence and energies and the logically necessary deduction that grace is a created phenomenon.[42] If man is not deified by the unmediated divine energies of God, then all that is left for man is an external, moral, and legal relationship with God. Metropolitan Hierotheos is quite explicit about the importance of this point:

[41] "Once it is admitted that Christ left the Church the power to forgive sins (see PENANCE), the power of granting indulgences is logically inferred. Since the sacramental forgiveness of sin extends both to the guilt and to the eternal punishment, it plainly follows that the Church can also free the penitent from the lesser or temporal penalty." Kent, "Indulgences" in the *Catholic Encyclopedia*.

[42] "Moreover, sanctifying grace as an active reality, and not a merely external relation, must be philosophically either substance or accident. Now, it is certainty not a substance which exists by itself, or apart from the soul, therefore it is a physical accident inhering in the soul, so that the soul becomes the subject in which grace inheres; but such an accident is in metaphysics called quality (*qualitas, poiotes*) therefore sanctifying grace may be philosophically termed a 'permanent, supernatural quality of the soul', or, as the Roman Catechism (P. II, cap. ii, de bap., n. 50) says 'divina qualitas in anima inhaerens'." J. Pohle, "Sanctifying Grace" in the *Catholic Encyclopedia*.

SALVATION

In fact, if one examines carefully all the differences between the Latins and the Orthodox, one will see clearly that they come down to one, to the truth concerning the essence and energy of God.[43]

In the previous chapter we saw that the doctrine of the *Filioque* was based on a philosophical approach to God. Likewise, the Roman Catholic Church has reduced the notion of salvation to a legal transaction modeled on Roman law. In both cases, Roman doctrine results from an over reliance on *speculative* theology.

There are, even in our day, holy men and women who have experienced the divine and deifying energies of God. There are those who have been beheld within the light of the Transfiguration. The Orthodox rejection of the Roman doctrines of satisfaction, merit, and the rest is based not on a love of contentiousness but on a love of the truth — truth discovered through experience. Orthodox and Roman Catholics do not simply use different words for the same reality, we experience *different* realities. This cannot help but affect the way we view the Christian life and the nature of the Church:

If, however, God were essence, or being alone, without His divine energies, if grace were a created thing — as Western Scholastics tell us — then man would be incapable of knowing Him directly, of

[43]*Life after Death*, p.181. Archimandrite George concurs: "If the Roman Catholics do not accept God's Grace as uncreated, we cannot be reconciled with them even if they acknowledge all the rest. After all, how will deification be accomplished, if divine Grace is created and not Uncreated energy of the All-holy Spirit?" *The Deification as the Purpose of Man's Life*, p. 35.

103

seeing Him, of becoming a God himself, for a created thing (grace) cannot deify the creature (man). Neither could God Himself be present within creation, nor could He be personally at work within it.[44] Just as the relentless laws of nature must replace an uncreated joy not present in nature, even so the absence of uncreated grace from the life of the Church and of Christians creates a need for an ethical and legal system whose head is the Pope.[45]

---

[44]This point is stressed by St. Gregory Palamas in *The One Hundred and Fifty Chapters,* esp. §99-§103.

[45]Archimandrite George (Capsanis), *The Eros of Repentance,* pp. 23-24.

The Church

Shun divisions, as the beginning of evils. All of you follow the bishop, as Jesus Christ followed the Father, and the presbytery as the Apostles; respect the deacons as the ordinance of God. Let no one do anything that pertains to the Church apart from the bishop. Let that be considered a valid Eucharist which is under the bishop or one whom he has delegated. Wherever the bishop shall appear, there let the people be; just as wherever Christ Jesus may be, there is the Catholic Church (St. Ignatius of Antioch, To the Smyrnaeans, 8).

Discussions of Orthodox-Roman Catholic relations invariably center upon the papacy. Indeed, that is usually the first—and sometimes the only—issue discussed. In this volume, however, I have tried to demonstrate that the differences between the Orthodox and Roman Catholic Churches go far beyond outward structure and custom. Orthodoxy and Roman Catholicism represent two very different ways of approaching the mystery of God and of man's salvation.

For the Orthodox, theology is not a matter of rationally drawing conclusions from a set of revealed premises or postulates, but is an empirical endeavor—a reflection upon the experience of the uncreated grace of God. Therefore, ecclesiology is the product of experience, not abstract speculation.

Furthermore, while admitting that the *understanding* of a doctrine can develop and become more explicit over time, the Orthodox flatly deny that doctrine itself develops. This is no less true for ecclesiology than for any other doctrine. Rome maintains that the doctrine of the papacy is a legitimate development of doctrine. The Orthodox answer that the nature of the Church cannot change; if the pope was not an infallible, universal ordinary in the second century, he cannot be an infallible, universal ordinary now.

These two principles—the primacy of experience and the denial that the nature of the Christian experience can legitimately change or develop—mean that the life of the early Church possesses a normative character. Apostolic succession—though it is traced through the succession of bishops—does not refer to a succession of personal authority from one bishop to another, but to the fundamental *identity in faith and life* of one community with those that have preceded it.[1] For the Orthodox, therefore, the apostolicity of the Church implies both historical continuity and material identity with the original Church of Jerusalem and with those first communities established throughout the Roman Empire by the Apostles.

---

[1]For this reason the Orthodox Church has no trouble in dismissing the claims of the "apostolic succession" of vagante bishops.

A brief analysis of Church history will demonstrate that the ecclesiology of the Orthodox Church is fully consonant with the life of the early Church, while that of the Roman Catholic Church represents a clear change—to the Romans, a development, but to the Orthodox, an apostasy.[2]

The Structure and Nature of the Local Church

According to St. Paul, the Apostles went from place to place, appointing and ordaining leaders in the local Churches:

> For this cause left I thee in Crete, that thou shouldest set in order the things that are wanting, and ordain presbyters in every city, as I had appointed thee: If any be blameless, the husband of one wife, having faithful children not accused of riot or unruly. For a bishop must be blameless, as the steward of God; not selfwilled, not soon angry, not given to wine, no striker, not given to filthy lucre... (Titus 1:5-7).

This passage brings out two very important points for understanding how the early Church was organized. First of all, notice that the terms "presbyter"

---

[2]Fr. John Meyendorff puts the matter succinctly: "There is today, however, some agreement on one point: whether or not it was of divine origin, the Roman primacy, as it existed in the fifth century, was already the result of a development—a development which continued through the early Middle Ages to reach its apogee with the Gregorian reforms in the late eleventh century. It is, therefore, a matter of theological judgement whether this Western historical process—which was not really understood, or accepted in the East—was a legitimate one." *Imperial Unity*, p. 59.

and "bishop" are used interchangeably. This is true not
only for the New Testament, but for patristic literature
throughout the first two centuries—the *Letters* of St.
Ignatius of Antioch being a singular exception.[3] The
second point, to which we shall return below, is that
there is a clear distinction drawn between the Apostles,
who were traveling missionaries, and the presbyters
and bishops who were appointed by them to govern the
local Churches.

The interchangeability of the *terms* "bishop" and
"presbyter" has led Protestant historians—and a few
Roman Catholics, who seem to have adopted Protestant
assumptions about the early Church—to conclude that
the early Church had a fluid form of government and
that the rule of one bishop in a diocese[4] was the result
of gradual development.[5] This conclusion, however,
must be rejected on historical as well as theological
grounds.

[3]Cf. *I Clement* 44, St. Irenaeus of Lyons, *Against Heresies* III:2:2,
III:3:2).

[4]I am using "diocese" here in the modern sense of the word,
denoting a local Christian Church comprised of the laity,
deaconate, and presbytery, headed by the bishop. In the Roman
Empire, however, "diocese" referred to largest political divisions
within the Empire.

[5]For a typical Protestant interpretation see E. Glenn Hinson's
introduction to *I Clement* in *The Early Church Fathers* (Nashville, TN:
Broadman Press, 1980), pp. 37ff. The Roman Catholic scholar
Johann Auer seems to accept the idea that the "monarchical
episcopate" is a development of the second century. See Auer and
Ratzinger, *Dogmatic Theology*, vol. 8, *The Church: The Universal
Sacrament of Salvation*, trans. by Michael Waldstein (Washington:
CUA Press, 1993), p. 264. Cited hereafter as *The Church*.

A careful examination of the literature from the early Church demonstrates that while the authors of the New Testament and post-apostolic eras may have used "bishop" and "presbyter" interchangeably, the Church had a clear structure from the very beginning and that this structure was determined by the nature of the Church as a eucharistic community.[6] Two documents are of particular importance in this regard: *I Clement* and the *Apology* of St. Justin.

Around AD 96, St. Clement, third bishop of Rome, sent a letter to the Church at Corinth.[7] In this letter, he used "bishop" and "presbyter" interchangeably. However, in a very important passage, he describes the structure of the Church in terms of the Old Testament priesthood:

> He commanded us to celebrate sacrifices and services, and that it should not be thoughtlessly or disorderly, but at fixed times and hours. He has Himself fixed by His supreme will the places and persons whom He desires for these celebrations, in or-

---

[6]I discuss this issue in greater detail in *The Way: What Every Protestant Should Know About the Orthodox Church* (Salisbury, MA: Regina Orthodox Press, 1997), esp. Chapter 8, pp. 152-178.

[7]This letter is often cited as proof of papal supremacy. However, St. Clement's name is never mentioned in the letter; it was sent from "the Church that sojourns in Rome to the Church that sojourns in Corinth." We know that St. Clement wrote the letter only from later sources (e.g. Irenaeus). Furthermore, nowhere does St. Clement claim any rights over against the local Corinthian Church. It should also be noted that St. Ignatius of Antioch also sent letters of advice to other Churches, but this certainly does not imply supremacy of the See of Antioch.

der that all things may be done piously according to His good pleasure, and be acceptable to His will. . . . For to the high priest his proper ministrations are allotted, and to the priests the proper place has been appointed, and on levites their proper services have been imposed. The layman is bound by the ordinances for the laity.[8]

This passage evinces a clear, four-fold Church structure: high priest (bishop), priests (presbyters), levites (deacons), and the laity. Notice also that these four offices are determined by their liturgical roles in the life of the Church.

Writing in the middle of the second century, St. Justin describes a structure identical to that described by St. Clement:

At the end of prayers we embrace each other with a kiss. Then bread is brought to the president of the brethren, and a cup of water and wine: this he takes, and offers praise and glory to the Father of all, through the name of His Son and of the Holy Spirit; and he gives thanks at length for our being granted these gifts at his hand. When he has finished the prayers and the thanksgiving (Eucharist) all the people present give their assent with *Amen*, a Hebrew word signifying "So be it." When the president has given thanks and all the people have assented, those whom we call "deacons" give a portion of the bread over which thanksgiving has been offered, and of the wine and

---

[8]*First Epistle of Clement.*

water, to each of those who are present; and they carry them away to those who are absent.[9]

Notice that St. Justin refers to the bishop as the "president" of the brethren. Now an assembly can have only one president. The reason for this is derived from the Eucharist itself, for someone must *preside* at the supper, offering the thanksgiving (Eucharist) to God.

This passage explains how the writers of the early Church could use "bishop" and "presbyter" interchangeably and yet describe a Church structure governed by a single person (bishop). The bishop is the "presiding presbyter" in the community—a position necessitated by the eucharistic nature of the community.[10]

This leads to an important question: Was the office of bishop—the presiding presbyter—held by one person exclusively, or did it rotate among the presbyters, similar to the concept of an "officer of the day"? While the latter is *theoretically* possible, all of the extant historical evidence points to the former. Indeed, *all* lists of apostolic succession from the early Church trace the succession of a *single* bishop in each Church.[11] Had the position of bishop (president) rotated among the presbytery, then no such lists would be possible.

With this background we can see that the ecclesiology of St. Ignatius of Antioch (c. AD 107) was in no way exceptional, though his clear and

[9]*First Apology* I:65.
[10]Cf. Zizioulas, p. 195.
[11]It is from St. Irenaeus' list that we know that Clement was the third bishop of Rome.

111

unambiguous use of "bishop" and "presbyter" was. He wrote:

> Take great care to keep one Eucharist. For there is one flesh of our Lord Jesus Christ and one cup to unite us by His blood; one sanctuary, as there is one bishop, together with the presbytery and the deacons, my fellow-servants. Thus all of your acts may be done accordingly to God's will.[12]

St. Ignatius' *terminology* would eventually be adopted by the whole Church, but—and I cannot stress this strongly enough—the basic *structure* he describes is identical to that described, in less precise language, by Ss. Clement and Justin.

Significantly, St. Ignatius also discusses the structure of the Church within the context of the Eucharist. For him, as well as for Ss. Clement and Justin, the governing structure of the Church is manifest in the worship of the Church. Metropolitan John Zizioulas summarizes the patristic evidence:

> As far as we can reconstruct this structure from the pieces of evidence that we possess, we can see that in the center of the *synaxis* [Greek for "gathering together" —C.C.] of the "whole Church" and behind the "one altar" there was the throne of the "one bishop" seated "in the place of God" or understood as the living "image of Christ." Around his throne were seated the presbyters, while by him stood the deacons helping him in the celebration, and in front of him the "people of God," that *order* of the church

---

[12]*To the Philadelphians* 4. Cf. also the passage from *To the Smyrnaeans* 8, quoted at the beginning of this chapter.

which was constituted by virtue of the rite of initiation (baptism-chrismation) and considered the *sine qua non* condition for the eucharistic community to exist and express the Church's unity.[13]

It is also significant that St. Ignatius is the first person to use the adjective "catholic" in regard to the Church. Here, again, I must stress that "catholic" does not mean "universal," but "whole, complete."[14] For St. Ignatius, the local Church—what we would call the diocese today—is the Catholic Church, for there, in the midst of the eucharistic assembly, presided over by the bishop, the fullness of Christ is manifested.[15] This is the very heart of the Orthodox understanding of the Church.

The Church and the Churches

If, however, each local Church is catholic, manifesting the plenitude of the life in Christ, then how are these catholic Churches related to one another? Is this not a recipe for congregationalism? Fr. Alexander Schmemann explains:

It must be stated emphatically that this type of ecclesiology does not transform the local Church into a self-sufficient monad, without any "organic" link with other similar monads. There is no

[13]Zizioulas, pp. 152-153.
[14]"Ecumenical" is the word Greek speakers would have used for "universal."
[15]Cf. Zizioulas, p. 143, n. 3.

"congregationalism" here. The organic unity of the Church universal is not less real than the organic unity of the local church. But if universal ecclesiology interprets it in terms of "parts" and "whole," for eucharistic ecclesiology the adequate term is that of *identity*: "the Church of God abiding in..." The Church of God is the one and indivisible Body of Christ, wholly and indivisibly present in each Church, i.e. in the visible unity of the people of God, the Bishop and the Eucharist. And if universal unity is indeed *unity of the Church* and not *merely unity of Churches,* its essence is not that all Churches together constitute one vast, unique organism, but that each Church—in the identity of order, faith and the gifts of the Holy Spirit—is the *same* Church, the same Body of Christ, indivisibly present wherever is the "ecclesia." It is thus the same organic unity of the Church herself, the "Churches" being not complementary to each other, as parts or members, but each one and all of them together being nothing else, but the One, Holy, Catholic, and Apostolic Church.[16]

This fundamental identity in faith and life of the individual catholic Churches guarantees the unity of all of them together. This means that the unity of the worldwide Church is neither secured by nor dependent upon any particular super-diocesan structure. However, this worldwide unity is *expressed* by the intercommunion of the Churches and by the

---

[16]Alexander Schmemann, "The Idea of Primacy in Orthodox Ecclesiology," in *The Primacy of Peter,* p. 40.

concelebration of the sacramental heads of these Churches with one another.[17]

Our Lord prayed that His followers might be one even as He and His Father are one. The mystery of the unity of the Church is, therefore, a Trinitarian mystery. Just as each person of the Trinity is "catholic" — that is, possesses the fullness (plenitude) of the divine nature, without being a "part" of a greater whole — so each local Church is catholic, possessing and manifesting the fullness of life in Christ in communion with all of the other Catholic Churches. The local Church, however, can in no way be regarded as part of a greater whole. This would be tantamount to saying that the Son is only part of God. At the same time, this identity implies a necessary communion and even order (τάξις) between the Churches.

Historically, the bishops of Churches in a given geographic area met together to discuss issues of common concern. Apostolic Canon 34 provides for just such a synodal structure, under the chairmanship of the bishop of the major city (metropolis) of the area. It is important to note that the metropolitan did not "rule over" the other bishops of the synod. The bishops ruled their own Churches, but issues of common concern as well as conflicts were brought to the synod. As chairman, the metropolitan had only one vote — as did the other bishops — although he did have "veto" privileges over the decisions of the synod:

[17]This is also expressed in canon law by the fact that a new bishop must be consecrated by at least two other bishops.

The bishops of every nation must acknowledge him who is first among them and account him as their head, and do nothing of consequence without his consent; but each may do those things only which concern his own parish [i.e. diocese—C.C.], and the country places which belong to it. But neither let him (who is the first) do anything without the consent of all; for so there will be unanimity, and God will be glorified through the Lord in the Holy Spirit.

It was only natural that these synods should be organized along the lines of the political divisions of the Roman Empire and that the bishops of the major cities—the centers of economic and political activity— should be given primacy. Eventually, the bishops of the major cities of the Empire gained primacy in their respective areas.[18]

Interestingly, apostolic foundation was *not* a major factor in determining primacy in the early Church.[19] No Church—not even Rome—could claim a stronger apostolic foundation than the Church of Jerusalem, yet it remained under the presidency of the metropolitan of

[18]Commenting on a similar ancient canon (Antioch, Canon 9), Dvornik notes, "This canon also recalls the reason which made the position of the metropolitans so important: because since all the political, economical and social life was concentrated in the capital, all those who had business to conduct were obliged to go there." *Byzantium*, p. 32.

[19]"...it was not apostolic origin which was the determining factor in the organization of the primitive Church. It was rather the principle of accommodation to the political organization of the Empire that was paramount." Dvornik, *Byzantium*, p. 31.

Caesarea until it was elevated to the status of a patriarchate by the Council of Chalcedon in 451.

Canon 28 of the Council of Chalcedon also elevated the see of Constantinople to second place behind that of Rome. The reason given was quite straightforward; Constantinople was now the capital of the Empire:

> Following in all things the decisions of the holy Fathers, and acknowledging the canon, which has been just read, of the One Hundred and Fifty Bishops beloved-of-God (who assembled in the imperial city of Constantinople, which is New Rome, in the time of the Emperor Theodosius of happy memory), we also do enact and decree the same things concerning the privileges of the most holy Church of Constantinople, which is New Rome. For the Fathers rightly granted privileges to the throne of old Rome, because it was the imperial city. And the One Hundred and Fifty most religious Bishops, actuated by the same consideration, gave equal privileges to the most holy throne of New Rome, justly judging that the city which is honoured with the Sovereignty and the Senate, and enjoys equal privileges with the old imperial Rome, should in ecclesiastical matters also be magnified as she is, and rank next after her...

Although it did not provoke a schism at the time, Rome never accepted this canon. The reasons *why* go to the heart of the differences between the ecclesiologies of the Roman Catholic and Orthodox Churches.

CHAPTER FOUR

Primacy According to Rome

The Orthodox Church has never denied that the Church of Rome possesses a certain primacy among the major sees of the world. The reason for this is clearly stated in Canon 28: "because it was the imperial city." As we saw above, regional primacies within the early Church were established on the same principle: the socio-political importance of the major city in the region. Because the imperial capital had been moved from Rome to Constantinople, the Fathers of Chalcedon granted to Constantinople—New Rome—privileges equal to those of Old Rome and second place in the order of Churches behind Rome, ahead of Alexandria, Antioch, and Jerusalem.

The Roman Church refused to accept this canon because, by this time (mid fifth century), Rome had come to have a different understanding of her place in the worldwide Church. She claimed that her primacy was not merely one of honor and special privileges pertaining to inter-church relations, but a primacy of jurisdiction over the ecumenical Church, based upon the pope's position as the unique successor to St. Peter. Implicit in this position are several assumptions:

1. The ecumenical or worldwide Church is the whole (Catholic) Church. The dioceses are related to the universal Church as parts to a whole. [20]

[20]"The individual *bishops* are the visible source and foundation of the unity in their own particular Churches" (*Lumen Gentium* 23). As such, they "exercise their pastoral office over the portion of the People of God assigned to them" (*Lumen Gentium* 23), assisted by

118

2. The bishops of the local Churches are the successors to the Apostles.[21]

3. As Peter was the "Prince of the Apostles" and leader of the college of Apostles, so his successor is the head of the universal Church.[22]

The Church of Rome has a universal primacy of jurisdiction over the ecumenical Church because her bishop is the sole successor of St. Peter. Rome, therefore, rejected Canon 28 of Chalcedon not merely because she felt threatened by Constantinople's new position, but because the very granting of "status" by

priests and deacons. But, as a member of the episcopal college, each bishop shares in the concern for all the Churches (Cf. *Christus Dominus* 3). The bishops exercise this care first "by ruling well their own Churches as portions of the universal Church," and so contributing "to the welfare of the whole Mystical Body, which, from another point of view, is a corporate body of Churches." *Catechism of the Catholic Church*, §886.

[21]"'Just as the office which the Lord confided to Peter alone, as first of the apostles, destined to be transmitted to his successors, is a permanent one, so also endures the office, which the apostles received, of shepherding the Church, a charge destined to be exercised without interruption by the sacred order of bishops' (*Lumen Gentium* 20 § 2). Hence the Church teaches that 'the bishops have by divine institution taken the place of the apostles as pastors of the church, in such wise that whoever listens to them is listening to Christ and whoever despises them despises Christ and him who sent Christ' (*Lumen Gentium* 20 § 2)." *Catechism of the Catholic Church*, §862.

[22]"The pope's primacy over the whole Church, as we showed above, is founded upon the succession of Peter. It is a unique primacy, just as there was only one Peter in the college of Apostles." Auer, *The Church*, p. 265.

an Ecumenical Council undercut Rome's unique claim to apostolic authority.

Let us take each of these ideas in order. We saw above that for St. Ignatius, the local Church is the Catholic Church. This was true, in general, for ecclesiastical writers until the late fourth and early fifth centuries, when the word came to mean "universal." Zizioulas notes:

> It was probably only in the fourth century and out of the struggle of such theologians as Optatus of Milevis (*Adv. Parm.*, 2,1) and Augustine (*Ep.*, XCIII, 23; *De Unite.*, 6, 16, etc.) against the provincialism of the Donatists that the term "catholic" came to be identified with "universal."[23]

The claim of the Roman pope to have universal ordinary jurisdiction over the worldwide Church is dependent upon the notion that the universal Church — rather than the diocese — is the Catholic Church. This however, is clearly at variance with the way early Christian writers saw things. For Latin writers such as Tertullian[24] and St. Cyprian[25], as well as for Greek writers such as St. Ignatius, the term "catholic" referred primarily to the local Church.[26] Whether one sees the equation of the "Catholic Church" with the "universal

---

[23]Zizioulas, p. 143-144, n3.

[24]See *Praescr. Haer.*, 26:4.

[25]According to O. Casel, the title of Cyprian's masterwork, *On the Unity of the Catholic Church*, refers to the local Church, not the universal Church. *Revue Bénédictine* 30 (1913), pp. 413-420.

[26]I am referring here to writers who wrote in the Latin or Greek languages, not to their ethnicity or nationality.

Church" as a development or degeneration, one cannot deny that this view represents a *change* from the way the early Christians understood the nature of the Church.

I should also point out that such a view distorts the Trinitarian nature of the Church described above. It is, in a very real way, analogous to the doctrine of the *Filioque*, which exalts the one divine nature at the expense of the catholicity of the persons.[27]

The second pillar of Rome's claim to universal jurisdiction is the identification of the bishops with the Apostles. We saw above in the passage from Titus that the Apostles went from place to place appointing the leadership of the local Churches. A clear distinction between the two is implicit in that passage. The Apostles were not bishops of the local Churches, but travelling missionaries. Furthermore, the bishops did not receive from the Apostles an "apostleship," but the grace to lead the local communities. The evidence for this is abundant.

First of all, we have only to look at the Mother of all Churches, Jerusalem. St. James was not considered to be an Apostle by the early Christians, but the first bishop of Jerusalem.[28] Significantly, at the first Church council

[27]It would be interesting to discover what influence, if any, St. Augustine's dependence on Neo-Platonism had on his identification of "catholic" with "universal." There may indeed be an historical, as well as conceptual, link between the Filioque an ' the Roman Catholic doctrine of the Church.

[28]Cf. Nicolas Koulomzine, "Peter's Place in the Early Church" in *The Primacy of Peter in the Orthodox Church* (The Faith Press, 1973/since reprinted by SVS Press), p.128.

(Acts 15), James, the bishop of the Jerusalem Church, presided, not St. Peter. It was James, not Peter, who issued the final decision.

Furthermore, the earliest succession lists for the Churches do not list the Apostles as the first bishops. According to Irenaeus, Linus, not Peter, was the first bishop of Rome.[29] This point has been repeatedly stressed by the Orthodox.[30] The clear distinction between Apostle and bishop was not unique to the East, however, for it was accepted without argument in Rome as well:

> The idea that the Apostles were, above all others, the teachers and masters sent by the Lord to preach the Gospel throughout the world was equally well rooted in Rome as it was universally accepted in the East. It is for this reason that the first Christians were not accustomed to designate an Apostle as the first bishop of the see where he had implanted the faith. The one who was considered the first bishop

[29] *Against Heresies* III:3:3.

[30] A rather late tradition developed in Constantinople naming St. Andrew as the founder and first bishop of Constantinople (Byzantium). This was clearly in reaction to Rome's claim of Petrine foundation and succession. St. Andrew was, after all, the "first-called." The claim that St. Andrew was the first bishop of Constantinople is not only historically weak, it runs counter to the traditional Orthodox understanding. Even in the late Middle Ages, however, well after the notion had gained some currency, Orthodox theologians continued to stress the difference between the office of Apostle and that of bishop. See Meyendorff, "St. Peter in Byzantine Theology," in *The Primacy of Peter in the Orthodox Church*, p. 22.

was the one who had been ordained by an Apostle. This custom was equally the practice in Rome.[31]

Thus, in the early Church—even in Rome—it would have been impossible to base a theory of primacy on the idea of succession from a particular Apostle, because bishops were not considered to be the successors of particular Apostles. According to Dvornik, St. Cyprian was the first to identify Apostle and bishop.[32] Indeed, the writings of Cyprian are pivotal—although *not* for the reasons commonly believed.

St. Cyprian left no doubt about the fact that the unity of the Church is founded on the unique ministry—the "Chair"—of St. Peter. In the first version[33] of *On the Unity of the Catholic Church* he writes:

> And although He assigns a like power to all the Apostles, yet He founded a single Chair, thus establishing by His own authority the source and hallmark of the [Church's] oneness. No doubt the others were all that Peter was, but a primacy is given to Peter, and it is [thus] made clear that there

[31]Dvornik, *Byzantium*, pp. 40-41.

[32]*Byzantium*, p. 42.

[33]There are two versions of Chapter 4 and numerous interpretations about which is the original and who created the second version and why. I am following here the thesis of Maruice Bévenot, S.J., put forth in the introduction to his English translation. He argues that Cyprian himself revised the text because it had been misinterpreted in Rome as a justification for universal jurisdiction, which Cyprian certainly did not teach. *St. Cyprian: The Lapsed—The Unity of the Catholic Church, Ancient Christian Writers* 25 (New York: Newman Press, 1957), pp. 5-8.

CHAPTER FOUR

is but one Church and one Chair. So too, even if
they are all shepherds, we are shown but one flock
which is to be fed by all the Apostles in common
accord. If a man does not hold fast to this oneness
of Peter, does he imagine that he still holds the
faith? If he deserts the Chair of Peter upon whom
the Church was built, has he still confidence that he
is in the Church?[34]

It is easy to see why apologists for Roman Catholic
ecclesiology trot out St. Cyprian as proof of Roman
primacy in the early Church. However, even Roman
Catholic scholars admit that Cyprian was
misunderstood and his teachings misapplied. Cyprian
was not talking about the unity of the universal Church,
but the unity of the local Church. The reference to the
Chair of Peter is not a reference to Rome alone, but to
the bishops in *each* local Church. The Jesuit scholar
Bévenot explains:

> The whole context is against restricting the meaning
> to 'the see of Rome.' Cyprian's argument is based
> on the unicity of the *origin* (in Peter) of Church and
> authority alike. The one authority was perpetuated
> in the legitimate successions of the bishops, and to
> break with one's bishop was to break with the one,
> Christ-established, authority, that is, the 'Chair of
> Peter.' Thus his argument was pertinent not only
> for Rome, where Novatian had broken with
> Cornelius (whose 'chair' was Peter's in a double
> sense), but also nearer home, where Felicissimus
> and his faction were in revolt against himself.

[34]*De Unitate* 4, Bévenot, pp. 49-50.

However, for those who recognized the true primacy of the see of Rome, Cyprian's words (taken out of their context) would naturally express the necessity of communion with Rome. It is not unreasonable to suppose (until proof of the contrary is forthcoming) that such an interpretation, put upon his words at the time of the baptismal controversy, led Cyprian to revise this chapter for its final edition.[35]

St. Cyprian affirms in the very next chapter: "The authority of the bishops forms a unity, of which each holds his part in its totality."[36] Each local bishop, therefore, holds the "Chair of Peter" in its entirety. The local bishop, the successor of Peter in each Church, is the center of unity in each local Church.

Although St. Cyprian's identification of the local bishop with St. Peter is unusual for his time, and in this regard represents a real departure from previous writers, the substance of his ecclesiology is identical to that of the theologians we have discussed above. Cyprian does not conceive of the Catholic Church as a worldwide entity headed by one man, the sole successor of Peter, but as the local Church, organized around the bishop, who, together with all of the other catholic bishops of the world, shares in the "Chair of Peter." It is the identity of these Churches, expressed in the identity of the one "Chair of Peter," that constitutes the unity of the universal Church.

[35]pp. 104-105, n30.
[36]*De Unitate* 5; Bévenot, p. 47.

Roman Catholic apologists, however, take this identification of the local bishop with St. Peter and use it as the basis for their *exclusive* identification of the bishop of Rome with Peter. Although Bévenot recognizes that this is *not* what Cyprian meant, he nonetheless sees in Cyprian's writings a stage in the *development* of the idea of Roman primacy:

> If the foregoing reconstruction is correct, we have in Cyprian's *De ecclesiae catholicae unitate* a good example of what a dogma can look like while still in an early stage of its development. The reality (in this case, the Primacy of Rome) is there all the time: it may be recognized by some; by others it may even be denied, and that though much of what they say or do unconsciously implies it.[37]

What Bévenot states here with such confidence is precisely the question at hand: does St. Cyprian's ecclesiology really *imply* the later Roman notion of universal primacy and jurisdiction? Was Cyprian "unconsciously" implying the modern doctrine of the papacy when he stood Pope Stephen down over the question of the baptism of heretics? Or, is the later development of the theory of Roman primacy an *illegitimate* development of Cyprian's thought? If Cyprian's ecclesiology is perfectly consonant with that of the other early Fathers and with that of the later Orthodox Fathers, and, if as Bévenot himself notes, Cyprian never implied that the bishop of Rome had "a

[37]p. 8.

real authority over the whole Church,"[38] then in what way can the modern doctrine of the papacy be said to be a *legitimate* development of his doctrine?

Auer states, "It is no longer possible today to join Cyprian in seeing the Petrine succession in the bishop of each local Church."[39] However, he gives no reason for this other than the fact that the Roman Catholic Church has developed a *different* ecclesiology from that of St. Cyprian.

The third pillar of Roman Catholic ecclesiology is that the bishop of Rome is the *unique* successor of St. Peter and as such is the head of the universal Church:

> The *Pope*, Bishop of Rome and Peter's successor, "is the perpetual and visible source and foundation of the unity both of the bishops and of the whole company of the faithful" (*Lumen Gentium* 23). "For the Roman Pontiff, by reason of his office as Vicar of Christ, and as pastor of the entire Church has full, supreme, and universal power over the whole Church, a power which he can always exercise unhindered" (*Lumen Gentium* 22; cf. *Christus Dominus* 2, 9).[40]

We saw above that the Fathers of the Council of Chalcedon cited the socio-political importance of Rome as the reason for Rome's primacy. The Roman Catholic historian Francis Dvornik refers to this method of inter-church organization as "Accomodation," meaning that the Church accommodated Her structure to the socio-

---

[38]p. 7.
[39]*The Church*, p. 287.
[40]*Catechism of the Catholic Church*, §882, p. 234.

political situation of the Roman Empire. Dvornik goes on to state, however, that this principle was originally accepted in Rome as well as in the East:

> We have seen that the principle of accommodation to the political division of the Empire was also accepted in Rome. And there is something more. When the civil diocese of Italy was divided in two as a result of the organization ordained by Diocletian, Milan became the capital of the diocese of *Italia annonaria* which comprised all of the north of Italy and the Bishop of Milan then assumed direct jurisdiction over all the provinces of the new diocese. The direct jurisdiction of the Bishop of Rome was limited to the provinces known as suburbicarian. Rome seems to have accepted this situation without protest because it agreed with the principle of accommodation to the division of the Empire.[41]

Thus, for the first three centuries of the Christian era, Rome accepted the principle that the super-diocesan structure of the Church would conform to the political divisions of the Roman Empire and that her own unique place in this arrangement was due to the fact that Rome was the capital and imperial residence. Once again, whether one considers it a development or a degeneration, Rome's position on her role in the universal Church *changed* over time. Rome did not

---

[41]*Byzantium*, p. 36. Dvornik is referring to the dioceses of the Roman Empire, that is, to the largest political divisions in the Empire. He is not using diocese in the modern sense as the local Church.

always assert universal jurisdiction, and she did not always base her claim on the succession of Peter.

Historians agree that this change was brought about by the social and political events of the fourth and fifth centuries, in particular the transfer of the imperial residence to Constantinople and the collapse of the Empire as a political institution in the West. Both Dvornik and Meyendorff emphasize the impact of the move of the capital.[42] The *Decretum Gelasianum* of the late fourth century explicitly opposes the apostolic authority of Rome against the pretensions of Constantinople: "The holy Roman church was placed at the head of the other churches not by some council, but it received primacy through the words of our Lord and Savior: *Thou art Peter...*"[43]

With the collapse of the political structure of the Western Roman Empire, the see of Rome became the only harbor of stability in a sea of confusion. Furthermore, Rome's status as the only Church in the West of apostolic foundation only magnified her importance. Auer explains:

> For this reason, the development of the doctrine of primacy, especially since the early Middle Ages, focused on the question of Peter's relation to his fellow apostles, of the pope's relation to the bishops. Let us sketch this development a little, since an understanding of the doctrines defined at the First Vatican Council depends upon an

[42]Dvornik, *Byzantium*, p. 42; Meyendorff, *Imperial Unity*, pp. 61ff.

[43]Quoted in Meyendorff, *Imperial Unity*, p. 62.

understanding of this development. Of great importance was the political and the related economic and social development of the Roman episcopal see after Constantine. This development was occasioned by the development of the Western Roman empire; by the absence of the Western Roman emperor from Rome (his residence was in Ravenna); by the weakness of the last Western Roman emperors and their eventual downfall; and by the advance of the Germanic peoples and their rule in Italy. For the bishops of Rome, whose Church had grown above all from the blood of the martyrs, these developments were not only an occasion but a call, the call of a historic moment to political action in the world in the service of the Church.[44]

Modern Roman Catholic apologists are fond of accusing the Christian East of caesaropapism. The super-diocesan structure of the Orthodox Church is, according to this view, but an example of the supremacy of the Empire over the Church in the East. This is contrasted with the "theological" doctrine of papal supremacy, founded on Christ's words to St. Peter. However, as we have pointed out several times in our study, Roman Catholic historians themselves have been forced to admit that Rome did not always claim universal jurisdiction, nor did she always justify her actions by an appeal to a unique Petrine succession. Indeed, it was the socio-political upheaval of the fourth

[44]*The Church*, pp. 279-280.

and fifth centuries that brought about the change in the Roman perspective.

If this is the case—and Roman Catholic historians agree that it is—then the development of the Roman Catholic understanding of ecclesiology was *determined* by socio-political realities. Indeed, the "developed doctrine" of papal supremacy seems more like an *a posteriori* justification for Rome's political pretensions, rather than a consistently developed theological position.[45]

Again, historians of the early Church—Roman Catholic and Orthodox alike—are in general agreement about the basic facts. The Roman Catholic argument for the papacy rests squarely on the idea of development. We have seen, however, that what developed in Rome was an ecclesiology vastly different from that of the early Church.

---

[45]Indeed, it is Rome's insistence on the Church as a universal organization headed by one man that truly resembles the political structure of the Roman Empire. For the Orthodox, the super-diocesan organization of the universal Church along the lines of the political divisions of the Empire was a matter of practicality. It could have taken a different form provided that the truth of the fundamental *identity* and *equality* of each local, Catholic Church was preserved. Thus, one can understand Archimandrite Vasileios' comment, "If the Lord had wanted a merely administrative unity, with no further implications in terms of life and mystery, He could have provided as an image of the Church's unity the Roman Empire, saying, 'Father, I desire that the faithful may be united as the Roman empire is united.' However, He did nothing of the sort, but asked instead that the trinitarian 'even as' should be the measure of everything in the Church's life." *Hymn of Entry*, p. 47.

If, as the early Church believed, each local Church (diocese) *is* the Catholic Church, then all Churches and, therefore, all bishops are equal. The Greek, lay theologian Alexander Kalomiros explains this principle:

A bishop is called a patriarch when the church of which he is the shepherd is a patriarchate, and an archbishop when the church is an archdiocese. In other words, the respect and honor belongs to the local church, and by extension it is rendered to its bishop. The Church of Athens is the largest and, today, most important local church of Greece. For this reason the greatest respect belongs to her, and she deserves more honor than any other church of Greece. Her opinion has a great bearing, and her role in the solution of common problems is the most significant. That is why she is justly called an archdiocese. Consequently, the bishop of that church, because he represents such an important church is a person equally important and justly called an archbishop. He himself is nothing more than an ordinary bishop. In the orders of priesthood — the deacon, the presbyter, and the bishop — there is no degree higher than the office of the bishop. The titles metropolitan, archbishop, patriarch, or pope do not indicate a greater degree of ecclesiastical charism, because there is no greater sacramental grace than that which is given to the bishop. They only indicate a difference in prominence of the churches of which they are shepherds.[46]

[46]Alexander Kalomiros, *Against False Union*, trans. by George Gabriel (Seattle: St. Nectarios Press, 1990), pp. 55-56.

There is absolutely *no way* to legitimately derive the Roman Catholic doctrine of the papacy from such an ecclesiology. If the local Church is the Catholic Church, and if all bishops are equal, then the pope cannot have universal ordinary jurisdiction over the universal church. In short, the doctrine of the papacy destroys the very idea of the local Church. As we shall see below, this problem continues to plague the Roman Church, even in the wake of Vatican II.

The Vatican Councils

With the First Vatican Council (1870), the doctrine of the papacy reached its apex. We shall deal with the question of papal infallibility below; for now, let us continue to focus on the question of jurisdiction. In particular, I want to emphasize the fact that it is a *dogma* of the Roman Catholic Church that the pope, as bishop of Rome, possesses universal ordinary jurisdiction over the universal Church and over each and every local Church in particular:

> Wherefore we *teach and declare* that, by divine ordinance, the Roman church possesses a pre-eminence of ordinary power over every other church, and that this jurisdictional power of the Roman pontiff is both episcopal and immediate. Both clergy and faithful, of whatever rite and dignity, both singly and collectively, are bound to submit to this power by the duty of hierarchical subordination and true obedience, and this not only in matters concerning faith and morals, but also in

those which regard the discipline and government
of the church throughout the world.[47]

Lest anyone should miss the import of these words, the
Council immediately added: "This is the teaching of the
catholic truth, and no one can depart from it without
endangering his faith and salvation."

Such a view is wholly incompatible with Orthodox
ecclesiology. If, as the Orthodox contend, each Church
is the Catholic Church, then there can be no Church
"over" the other Churches, and there can never be *two*
bishops in a Church at the same time. If, however, each
local Church (diocese) has a bishop, and if the pope has
universal ordinary authority over each and every
Church, then either there are *two* bishops in each
place—the pope and the local bishop—or the pope is
the real bishop, and the local bishop is but the pope's
vicar. Vatican I tried to address this issue:

> This power of the supreme pontiff by no means
> detracts from that ordinary and immediate power
> of episcopal jurisdiction, by which bishops, who
> have succeeded to the place of the apostles by
> appointment of the holy Spirit, tend and govern
> individually the particular flocks which have been
> assigned to them. On the contrary, this power of
> theirs is asserted, supported and defended by the
> supreme and universal pastor; for St Gregory the
> Great says: "My honour is the honour of the whole
> church. My honour is the steadfast strength of my

[47]*Pastor Aeternus* 3.

brethren. Then do I receive true honour, when it is denied to none of those to whom honour is due."[48]

This statement simply cannot be reconciled with the affirmation of papal jurisdiction above. Two bishops cannot have immediate ordinary jurisdiction over the same (local) Church at the same time. As J. M. R. Tillard says, "One would like to know how, in practice, the power of the Roman pontiff is to promote rather than stifle that of the other bishops."[49]

Imagine what would happen if the president of the United States were to declare that he had immediate executive power over each and every state government and that this would in no way detract from the immediate executive authority of the governors. What would happen if the president and a governor disagreed on a matter of policy? Who would overrule whom? One person would have to have supreme authority. In the end, the governor would exercise "his" authority *only* at the pleasure of the president. In real terms, he would be no more than the vicar of the president. This is exactly the case with the Roman Catholic Church. The pope has supreme, immediate, ordinary authority, and—however much the authority

---

[48]*Pastor Aeternus* 3.

[49]*The Bishop of Rome,* trans. by John de Satgé (Wilmington, DE: Michael Glazier, Inc., 1983), pp. 27-28. Indeed, Tillard goes on to state that the Council *deliberately* avoided any explicit elucidation of the rights of the bishops because "the Deputation were afraid of anything that might expose the power of the head of the Church to encroachment from the bishops."

of the local bishop may be emphasized in rhetoric—the local bishop can be no more than the vicar of the real bishop, the pope. As if there could be any doubt about this, the Council went on to say:

> So, then, if anyone says that the Roman pontiff has merely an office of supervision and guidance, and not the full and supreme power of jurisdiction over the whole church, and this not only in matters of faith and morals, but also in those which concern the discipline and government of the church dispersed throughout the whole world; or that he has only the principal part, but not the absolute fullness, of this supreme power; or that this power of his is not ordinary and immediate both over all and each of the churches and over all and each of the pastors and faithful: let him be anathema.[50]

Roman Catholic scholars—even conservatives—recognize that Vatican I was very much the product of its age. Auer describes the cultural milieu in which the council took place:

> It was only in the nineteenth century that the deeper theological vision of the Church appeared again. The stimulus for this vision came probably from Romanticism, which possessed a more profound sense of the historical and mystical dimensions of existence (Tübingen school, J. A. Möhler). Another important stimulus was the great political conflict between the idea of the absolute ruler and state (F. W. Hengel) and democratic revolution (beginning with the French Revolution

[50]*Pastor Aeternus* 3.

in 1789), which again pushed the more political aspect into the foreground. These spiritual conflicts led to the first dogmatic definitions about the Church at the First Vatican Council (1870).[51]

As tempting as it is to discuss the influence of Romanticism on the development of Roman Catholic dogma, I want to highlight instead the conflict between authoritarianism and political liberalism. The growth of liberal democracy throughout the twentieth century — much of which was condemned in the *Syllabus of Errors*[52] — placed tremendous stress on the decidedly authoritarian decrees of Vatican I. If the First Vatican Council was the product of the late nineteenth century, then Vatican II was clearly the product of the mid twentieth century.

In addition to the pressures of an increasingly democratic culture, Vatican II was also influenced by ecumenical concerns.[53] Tillard notes, in particular, that Roman Catholics were finding a new interest in and

---

[51] *The Church*, pp. 281-282.

[52] The *Syllabus of Errors* was promulgated by Pope Pius IX in 1864. In this document he listed the errors of the modern, liberal culture. Error 77, for example, remonstrates against the belief that "In this our age it is no longer expedient that the Catholic religion should be treated as the only religion of the state, all other worships whatsoever being excluded." Colman J. Barry, O.S.B., ed., *Readings in Church History*, vol. 3, *The Modern Era 1789 to the Present* (New York: Newman Press, 1965), pp. 70ff.

[53] Auer cites the lack of ecumenical perspective as the greatest drawback of Vatican I. *The Church*, p. 284.

appreciation for Eastern Orthodoxy.[54] This new cultural/intellectual milieu gave rise to a fresh appraisal of ecclesiology by the bishops of Vatican II.

Tillard argues that while Vatican II "in no way changed the letter of *Pastor Aeternus*,"[55] Vatican I was seen within a new perspective: "Vatican I and Vatican II together form a dialectical unity in which one should be interpreted by the other."[56] Most importantly, the council balanced the doctrine of the papacy with an increased emphasis on the role of the bishops. Indeed, Vatican II specifically said that the bishops should *not* be viewed as merely vicars of the pope.[57] Tillard summarizes the importance of Vatican II:

> Such then is the place of the papacy according to Vatican II. It belongs to the episcopal ministry and must not be severed from its roots there. A dialectical tension exists at the heart of this ministry possessed by all the bishops with the bishop of Rome at the head of the college, and must be maintained: a tension between the local or particular pole and the universal pole; between the pole of plurality and the pole of unity whose interplay is the stuff of communion. This is what allows *Ecclesia catholica* to be present in *ecclesia*

[54]Tillard, p. 34. Tillard, a Dominican, was a friend of Fr. John Meyendorff.
[55]Tillard, p. 35.
[56]Tillard, p. 35.
[57]*Lumen Gentium* 27.

localis and *Ecclesia catholica* (*universalis*) to be built from the communion of the *ecclesiae locales.*[58]

Tillard is very sympathetic to the Orthodox view, and his interpretation of Vatican II reflects that. To the extent that Roman Catholics have come to an increased appreciation for the local Church and bishop, the Orthodox should be encouraged. However, as Tillard himself notes, "...*Lumen Gentium* never settled the difficult question of the boundaries in practice between the authority and power of the bishop of Rome and that of the other bishops..."[59] Again, "Vatican II thus gave no firm juridical norm, no canonically formulated limit which would make it quite clear how far the pope's powers extended."[60] Furthermore, *Christus Dominus*, which came after *Lumen Gentium*, strongly reasserts the powers of the pope.[61]

Furthermore, the practical attempts to increase the influence of the bishops have failed to yield real fruit. The Synod of Bishops is nothing more than an advisory board to the pope.[62] Indeed, John Paul II has, if

[58]Tillard, p. 41.
[59]Tillard, p. 41.
[60]Tillard, p. 42.
[61]Tillard also notes that *Patorale Munus* (1963) asserts that the pope "concedes" powers to the bishops.
[62]"The synod only exists in order to let the Roman pontiff know its opinion. It is not able to address the church directly so as to express, in communion with the pope but not simply preparing the pope's own decision, the judgement of the universal episcopate on the matters at issues. Its conclusions are addressed to the pope and it is for him to decide if they should be published and how." Tillard, p. 44.

anything, strengthened his own authority as the one Successor of Peter and Vicar of Christ. Recently, the pope *unilaterally* inserted several paragraphs into the Code of Canon Law *and* the Code of the Canons of the Eastern Churches.[63]

The question immediately arises, why has Vatican II not lived up to—what Tillard believes to be—its potential? The answer is to be found in Tillard's own analysis. However much Vatican II may have sought to balance the one-sidedness of Vatican I with an increased emphasis on the role of the diocesan bishops, however much the bishops at Vatican II may have tried to nuance the definition of papal authority by placing it in the context of the worldwide episcopate, Vatican II did not touch the substance of Vatican I. As long as Roman Catholic ecclesiology rests on the three pillars outlined above, then no real movement toward a true Orthodox-conciliar structure is possible.

Even Tillard, for all of his appreciation for Orthodoxy, still thinks of the Catholic Church as the *universal* Church: "This is what allows *Ecclesia catholica* to be present in *ecclesia localis* and *Ecclesia catholica*

---

[63]The Apostolic Letter, *Ad Tuendam Fidem*, was issued as a *Motu Proprio*, a statement issued in the pope's own name and authority. Significantly, the new paragraphs, which essentially crack down on dissent among Catholic theologians, apply to the Eastern Churches (Uniates) as well. This should be clear enough proof of Rome's supremacy over the Eastern Churches to anyone still laboring under the delusion that they are self-governing Churches "in communion" with Rome rather than exotic liturgical rites "in subjection" to Rome.

(*universalis*) to be built from the communion of the *ecclesiae locales*." Note the capitalization in this passage.

Pope John Paul II, in a letter to the bishops of Australia, stresses the importance of the local bishop:

> From the Second Vatican Council, the figure of the diocesan bishop emerged with new vigor and clarity. With your fellow bishops and in union with the Successor of Peter, you have by the power of the Holy Spirit received the task of caring for the Church of God, the Bride purchased at the cost of the Blood of the only-begotten Son, the Lord Jesus Christ (cf. *Acts* 20:28).[64]

He goes on, however, to locate this new found appreciation for the local bishop within the context of Vatican I ecclesiology:

> Since the particular Churches over which the individual bishops preside represent a portion of the People of God assigned to the bishop's pastoral governance, they are not complete in themselves but exist in and through communion with the one, holy, Catholic, and apostolic Church.

As long as the Catholic Church is conceived to be the universal Church, and the local Church but a portion of that, then there is no way to balance the God-ordained rights, privileges, and responsibilities of the local bishops with those of the "Head of the whole Church." Such an ecclesiology is simply incompatible with the Orthodox understanding of the Church, and

---

[64]*L'Osservatore Romano*, English edition, Dec. 16th, 1998.

no amount of "tweaking" it with Orthodox-friendly language or talk about a renewed interest in "Eucharistic Ecclesiology"[65] can change that fact. Tillard's talk of "rereading" Vatican I is, therefore, nonsense. Vatican I does not need to be reinterpreted, but repudiated. You cannot grow roses in a bed of asphalt, and you cannot derive an Orthodox understanding of the Church from a heretical one.

Infallibility

The Roman Catholic doctrine of the papacy leads naturally and inevitably toward the doctrine of infallibility. Promulgated at the First Vatican Council in 1870, this doctrine marks the apex of papal pretensions. The history of this doctrine and, in particular, the history of the deliberations at Vatican I are well documented.[66] Here, I shall focus on the most

[65]Eucharistic Ecclesiology is the academic name given to the understanding of the structure of the Church outlined above in the first part of this chapter. Its primary exponents are Frs. Nichaols Afanassieff, John Meyendorff, and Alexander Schmemann, and Metropolitan John Zizioulas. See esp. Zizioulas' *Being as Communion*. Roman Cathoics such as Tillard have shown a growing appreciation for this understanding of the Church. However, as noted above, this appreciation has failed to result in a substantive change in Roman Catholic ecclesiology.

[66]See especially August Bernhard Hasler, *How the Pope Became Infallible* (Garden City, NY: Doubleday and Co., 1981) and Brian Tierney, *Origins of Papal Infallibility 1150-1350: A Study on the Concepts of Infallibility, Sovereignty and Tradition in the Middle Ages* (Leiden: E. J. Brill, 1972). For a good Orthodox appraisal see Michael Whelton, *Two Paths: Papal Monarch — Collegial Tradition*

important aspect of the controversy for understanding ecclesiology.

Roman Catholic apologists insist that the infallibility of the pope is but a function of the infallibility promised by Christ to the Church. It is also present "in the body of bishops when, together with Peter's successor, they exercise the supreme Magisterium..."[67] However, Vatican I stated clearly:

> We teach and define as a divinely revealed dogma that when the Roman pontiff speaks *ex cathedra*, that is, when, in the exercise of his office as shepherd and teacher of all Christians, in virtue of his supreme apostolic authority, he defines a doctrine concerning faith or morals to be held by the whole church, he possesses, by the divine assistance promised to him in blessed Peter, that infallibility which the divine Redeemer willed his church to enjoy in defining doctrine concerning faith or morals. Therefore, such definitions of the Roman pontiff are of themselves, and not by the consent of the church, irreformable.[68]

This passage highlights the two central facets of this doctrine. First, the infallibility is *located* in a single

(Salisbury, MA: Regina Orthodox Press, 1998). For an insightful analysis of Vatican I from a contemporary Roman Catholic see John Emerich Edward Dalberg-Acton (Lord Acton), *Essays in Religion, Politics, and Morality. Selected Writings of Lord Acton,* vol. 3 (Indianapolis: Liberty Classics/Liberty Press, 1988), esp. pp. 263-391.

[67]*Lumen Gentium* 25, quoted in *The Catechism of the Catholic Church,* §891.

[68]*Pastor Aeternus* 4.

person, by virtue of his office. Second, this authority is derived, not from the consensus of the whole Church, but from the pope's own authority as the successor of Peter.

The Orthodox certainly believe that the Church, *qua* Church, is infallible. However, there has never been an attempt to locate that infallibility in any one person or institution. It is commonly said that the Ecumenical Councils are infallible. However, no council could claim to be infallible simply by virtue of its existence. Only after the decisions of a council are "received" by the Church at large, that is, after they are found to be in conformity with the mind of the Church (*consensus Ecclesiae*) can they be said to be infallible. Numerous "ecumenical" councils have been held, which were rejected by the faithful.[69]

If a council, simply by virtue of being called, cannot claim automatic infallibility, then certainly no one person in the Church can make such a claim. The Church does not err, but any member of the Church—even the most august bishops—may err. Peter was rebuked by St. Paul. Pope Honorius was condemned for heresy by an Ecumenical Council.[70] Pope John VIII

[69]Among these is the Robber Synod of 449. In an astounding display of arrogance and intellectual dishonesty, the drafters of *Pastor Aeternus* (Ch. 4) actually cite the Councils of Lyons and Florence—both rejected as false councils by the Orthodox—as proof of the universal acceptance of the doctrine of the papacy.

[70]The case of Honorius was to prove highly embarrassing to the proponents of papal infallibility. Lord Acton observed: "This inclination to get rid of evidence was specially associated with the doctrine of papal infallibility, because it is necessary that the Popes

condemned the *Filioque*, yet his decision, "irreformable" by the standards of Vatican I, was reversed by popes in the eleventh century.[71] If he was wrong, then he erred; if he was right, his successors (down to the present) erred.

For the Orthodox, the criterion for orthodoxy is the mind of the Church, the *consensus Ecclesiae*. However, Rome has clearly placed the pope *above* this consensus. If history does not support position—and it clearly does not—then why did the theory develop in the first place, and why do Roman Catholics still cling to it, even if—as Tillard attempts to do—they "reinterpret" it in light of their own perspectives?

themselves should not testify against their own claim. They may be declared superior to all other authorities, but not to that of their own see. Their history is not irrelevant to the question of their rights. It could not be disregarded; and the provocation to alter or to deny its testimony was so urgent that men of piety and learning became a prey to the temptation of deceit. When it was discovered in the manuscript of the *Liber Diurnus* that the Popes had for centuries condemned Honorius in their profession of faith, Cardinal Bona, the most eminent man in Rome, advised that the book should be suppressed if the difficulty could not be got over; and it was suppressed accordingly. Men guilty of this kind of fraud would justify it by saying that their religion transcends the wisdom of philosophers, and cannot submit to the criticism of historians. If any fact manifestly contradicts a dogma, that is a warning to science to revise the evidence. There must be some defect in the materials or in the method. Pending its discovery, the true believer is constrained humbly but confidently to deny the fact." pp. 309-310.

[71]See Chapter 1, above.

In *The Brothers Karamazov,* Ivan Karamazov spins a bizarre tale entitled, "The Grand Inquisitor."[72] In this tale, Christ comes back to earth—Seville, Spain—in the sixteenth century. He is imprisoned and interrogated by the Grand Inquisitor. The old man informs Christ that the [Roman Catholic] Church has improved on Christ's work. The freedom that Christ won for man is too much of a burden for him. Man does not want freedom, but "miracle, mystery, and authority." The Church has accepted the offer from the devil that Christ refused on the Temple mount and thereby has "corrected" Christ's work.

Ultimately, this need for an *ex officio* infallible pope is rooted in the *fear* of freedom and in the psychological need of fallen man for a secure authority. Tillard observes:

> The climate of ultramontane opinion which accompanied and to some extent brought about the definition of pontifical primacy in 1870 has marked the Catholic understanding of the papacy as deeply as if the two were to be identified. Catholic outlook, at the level even of spontaneous reactions from several episcopates, has come to look upon the pope with religious or simply emotional attitudes which sometimes obscure the essential characteristics of the bishop of Rome's function. Vatican II has hardly touched Catholic sentiment at this point. The rank

---

[72]Without question, the best English translation is Fyodor Dostoyevsky, *The Brothers Karamazov,* trans. by Richard Pevear and Larissa Volokhonsky (New York: Vintage Classics, 1990). For "The Grand Inquisitor," see pp. 246-274.

and file thirst for a papacy that will satisfy their taste for "marvels."[73]

The Protestant theologian Dietrich Bonhoeffer once quipped, "Verbal inspiration [of the Bible] is a poor substitute for the resurrection!"[74] An Orthodox Christian might add that an infallible pope is a poor substitute for the Holy Spirit.

[73]Tillard, p. 18.
[74]*Christ the Center*, trans. by Edwin H. Robertson (San Francisco: Harper and Row, 1978), p. 73.

CHAPTER FIVE

The Mother of God

> There is an equal harm in both these heresies,
> both when men demean the Virgin and when,
> on the contrary, they glorify her beyond what
> is proper (St. Epiphanius of Cyprus).

Marian devotion arose in the Christian East and spread to the West. It would seem, therefore, that if Roman Catholics and Orthodox could be united on any subject, it would be devotion to the Mother of God, the Mother of all Christians. Sadly, however, this is not the case. Just as the Roman Catholic Church added the *Filioque* to the creed and distorted the doctrine of the Trinity, just as she absolutized a one-sided view of the doctrine of salvation and developed it into a complex theology of merit, purgatory, and indulgences, and just as she distorted the fundamental unity-amidst-plurality of the early Church by turning the papacy into a universal monarchy, so Rome has also developed her teaching on the Mother of God into something far different from that held by the early Church.

The primary point of contention is the doctrine of the Immaculate Conception, defined as a dogma by Pope Pius IX in the bull *Ineffabilis Deus* (1854). As Orthodox are often accused of misrepresenting—or at

148

least misinterpreting—the doctrine, I will reproduce the relevant paragraph from the *Catholic Encyclopedia*:

In the Constitution *Ineffabilis Deus* of 8 December, 1854, Pius IX pronounced and defined that the Blessed Virgin Mary "in the first instance of her conception, by a singular privilege and grace granted by God, in view of the merits of Jesus Christ, the Saviour of the human race, was preserved exempt from all stain of original sin." The subject of this immunity from original sin is the person of Mary at the moment of the creation of her soul and its infusion into her body. The term *conception* does not mean the *active* or *generative* conception by her parents. Her body was formed in the womb of the mother, and the father had the usual share in its formation. The question does not concern the immaculateness of the generative activity of her parents. Neither does it concern the passive conception absolutely and simply (*conceptio seminis carnis, inchoata*), which, according to the order of nature, precedes the infusion of the rational soul. The person is truly conceived when the soul is created and infused into the body. Mary was preserved exempt from all stain of original sin at the first moment of her animation, and sanctifying grace was given to her before sin could have taken effect in her soul. The formal active essence of original sin was not removed from her soul, as it is *removed* from others by baptism; it was *excluded*, it never was simultaneously with the exclusion of sin. The state of original sanctity, innocence, and justice, as opposed to original sin, was conferred upon her, by which gift every stain and fault, all depraved emotions, passions, and debilities, essentially pertaining in her soul to original sin, were excluded. But she was not made exempt from the temporal penalties of Adam — from sorrow, bodily infirmities, and death. The immunity from original sin was given to Mary by a singular exemption from a universal law through the same merits of Christ, by which other men are cleansed from sin by baptism. Mary needed the redeeming Saviour to obtain this exemption, and to be delivered from the universal necessity and debt (*debitum*) of being subject to original sin. The person of Mary, in consequence of her origin from Adam, should have been subject to sin, but, being the new Eve who was to be the mother of the new Adam, she was, by the eternal counsel of God and by the merits of Christ, withdrawn from the general law of original sin. Her redemption was the very masterpiece of Christ's redeeming wisdom. He is a greater redeemer who pays the debt that it may not be incurred than he who pays after it has fallen on the debtor. Such is the meaning of the term "Immaculate Conception."[1]

This doctrine is fascinating for a number of reasons, not the least of which is the fact that it was opposed by some the Roman Catholic Church's most eminent theologians, including Bernard, Bonaventure, and Thomas Aquinas—all canonized saints of the Roman Church. Furthermore, as Hilda Graef points out in her exceptional *Mary: A History of the Doctrine and Devotion*, the leading early proponents of the doctrine, Eadmer

[1]From the article, "Immaculate Conception" by Frederick G. Holweck.

and Duns Scotus, were not canonized by the Church.[2] Indeed, for much of the late Middle Ages, the doctrine was a point of dispute between the Dominicans (followers of Aquinas) and the Franciscans (followers of Duns Scotus).

Clearly the doctrine of the Immaculate Conception is the result of "doctrinal development." Once again, however, the Orthodox do not view this as a legitimate development of the *expression* of doctrine, but as a change in the *substance* of theology. Not only is the Immaculate Conception a theological error, it opens the door for further "developments" that are even more objectionable.

Before we address the Orthodox objections, however, we must deal with one common misunderstanding in regard to the patristic sources. Roman Catholic apologists are fond of rifling through works of the early Fathers of the Church looking for passages (usually taken out of context) that support this or that Roman Catholic doctrine—much in the same way that Protestants are wont to find Bible verses that support whatever new idea happens to be in vogue that week. Thus in both the Catholic popular press and in some academic writings, one can find various Greek Fathers cited in support of the doctrine of the Immaculate Conception. In light of this, it is appropriate to quote

---

[2](Westminster, MD: Christian Classics, 1965), Part One, viii, n1. The edition I have contains parts one and two in a single volume, but pagination starts anew with the beginning of Part Two. All citations, therefore, will indicate the appropriate part.

Hilda Graef (a Roman Catholic), who sets the record straight:

> While in the West Marian doctrine and devotion developed considerably between the eleventh and fifteenth centuries, in the East they remained in some respects more static. For here the three influences that largely determined Western developments were absent: the Augustinian doctrine of original sin, which played such a decisive part in the controversy about the Immaculate Conception; an illiterate and often still semi-barbarian laity; and scholasticism. Most of the authors who will now be considered [Orthodox writers of the medieval period—C.C.] extolled Mary's purity in the highest terms and are therefore frequently cited as witnesses for the Immaculate Conception by Latin theologians, so for example by M. Jugie in his book *L'Immaculée Conception dans l'Écriture sainte et dans la tradition orientale* (Rome, 1952). In order to avoid too many repetitions I shall state at once that it seems to me that the whole question was seen by the Greeks in an altogether different light from that in which it was considered by Western theologians. In the Greek Church original sin had never played the same preponderant part as in post-Augustinian Western thought. From very early times it had been assumed as an indisputable fact that Mary was the purest creature imaginable, the highest angels not excepted. St. John of Damascus had even considered her active conception to have been without sin, but as he did not share the Augustinian view of original sin as an inherited guilt transmitted

through the sexual act, the problem never presented itself to him in the way it did to Latin theologians. For the Greeks saw original sin far more as mortality with all its implications, and as the Theotokos was subject to this, they did not exempt her from it. On the other hand, though they affirmed Mary's complete purity, they were less interested than the Western theologians in the question of the precise moment when this had been established. We might almost say that the Latins considered the question from the historical, the Greeks from the metaphysical, point of view; the former were concerned about when this purity had begin, the latter were only interested in the fact that it existed. For this reason I do not think one can claim these Greek authors for the Immaculate Conception.[3]

Exemplar or Exception?

Fr. Alexander Schmemann once noted that the Immaculate Conception makes the Virgin Mary the "Great Exception" to humanity, not the "Great Exemplar." This is the first Orthodox objection to the doctrine: it sets the Mother of God apart from humanity not just in the degree of her purity, but qualitatively.

Theologians of both East and West praised and hymned the Virgin's purity. Indeed, on the whole, the hymnography of the East can be more flowery and exuberant in its rhetoric than that of the West. Everyone agreed, therefore, that the Virgin was pure, but how

[3]Part One, pp. 322-323.

and when did she get that way, and what implications does it have for how we view her? The starting point for the diverging of traditions was, as Graef so ably pointed out in the passage quoted above, the Augustinian definition of original sin as the guilt or the taint of Adam's sin that is passed on through sexual reproduction.[4] Thus, original sin is seen first and foremost as inherited guilt. Anselm of Canterbury would refine this somewhat, by redefining it as the absence of original justice. Although Anselm did not teach the Immaculate Conception—he specifically stated that Mary was born with original sin—Graef notes Anselm's unwitting role in the development of the idea:

> If Mary was the purest of all creatures, and if original sin was but the absence of original justice, then no more was needed than the anticipation of the effects of Christ's passion to make the Immaculate Conception theologically acceptable.[5]

This conclusion was drawn by Anselm's disciple, Eadmer, who wrote "the first detailed exposition of the doctrine of the Immaculate Conception."[6] He argued that if a chestnut could grow under thorns but not be harmed by them, then God could have made the Virgin to be conceived of sinful parents without herself being

[4]Cf. Jaroslav Pelikan, *Mary Through the Centuries: Her Place in the History of Culture* (New Haven: Yale University Press, 1996), pp. 189-191. Hereafter cited as *Mary*.
[5]Part One, p. 211.
[6]Graef, Part One, p. 218.

touched by sin. "He certainly could do it; if, therefore, he willed it, he did it."[7]

Of course, no Orthodox Christian would deny that God *could* do anything He wanted, but this begs the question entirely of whether or not he *did* do things this way.[8] For the Orthodox, man does not inherit the *guilt* for Adam's sin, but rather the *effects* of that sin, namely a nature enslaved to corruption and death.[9] Keep in mind that the Orthodox never developed the legalistic framework for understanding sin and salvation that developed in the Latin speaking West.

To say, then, that the Virgin was exempt from original sin is tantamount to saying that she was exempt from being human. Notice that in the explanation of the doctrine from the *Catholic Encyclopedia* it is stated that original sin was not *removed* from her, but excluded altogether. She was exempted from original sin and all of the passions that go along with it. Truly this makes her an exception to the human race, not its crowning glory.

For the Orthodox, Mary's glory lies precisely in the fact that she is a human *like* us, including a human nature subject to the passions. St. John (Maximovitch) of San Francisco writes:

> This teaching, which seemingly has the aim of exalting the Mother of God, in reality completely

[7]Quoted in Graef, Part One, p. 219.
[8]Cf. Pelikan, *Mary*, p. 196.
[9]See J. S. Romanides, "Original Sin According to St. Paul," in *St. Vladimir's Quarterly*, 4:1-2 (1955).

denies all Her virtues.... The righteousness and sanctity of the Virgin Mary were manifested in the fact that She, being "human with passions like us," so loved God and gave Herself over to Him, that by Her purity She was exalted high above the rest of the human race. For this, having been foreknown and forechosen, She was vouchsafed to be purified by the Holy Spirit Who came upon Her, and to conceive of Him the very Saviour of the world. The teaching of the grace-given sinlessness of the Virgin Mary denies Her victory over temptations; from a victor who is worthy to be crowned with crowns of glory, this makes Her a blind instrument of God's Providence.[10]

St. John brings out an important point here, if Mary was exempted from the passions, then her *fiat*—her *Let it be unto me according to thy word*—is meaningless. She was but a passive tool in the plan of salvation. Of course, Roman Catholics would deny this, yet it is the inevitable conclusion of the doctrine of the Immaculate Conception. Interestingly, Pope John Paul II's encyclical, *Redemptoris Mater*, was published in book form in the United States as *Mary, God's Yes to Man.*[11] For the Orthodox, however, Mary represents the perfect, free

---

[10]*The Orthodox Veneration of Mary the Birthgiver of God,* trans. by Fr. Seraphim Rose (Platina, CA: St. Herman of Alaska Brotherhood, 1994), pp. 59-60. In addition to St. John's critique, see also Fr. Michael Pomazansky, *Orthodox Dogmatic Theology: A Concise Exposition,* Trans. by Fr. Seraphim Rose (Platina CA: St. Herman of Alaska Brotherhood, 1994), pp. 192-195.

[11]Trans. by Lothar Krauth (Ignatius Press, 1988).

response of man to God. Her *fiat* is mankind's "Yes" to God:

> What shall we offer Thee, O Christ, Who for our sakes hast appeared on earth as man? Every creature made by Thee offers Thee thanks. The angels offer Thee a hymn; the heavens a star; the Magi, gifts; the shepherds, their wonder; the earth, its cave; the wilderness, the manger; and we offer Thee a Virgin Mother (*The Festal Menaion*)![12]

Errant Trajectory

In addition to the fact that the Immaculate Conception is based on a faulty understanding of original sin (and its attendant legalistic framework), and in addition to the fact that it makes the Virgin an exception to the human race, the Orthodox also object to the doctrine on the grounds that it would naturally lead to the exaltation of the Mother of God on a par with that of God Himself.

This tendency can already seen in those who first defended the doctrine. Eadmer said, "Sometimes salvation is quicker if we remember Mary's name than if we invoke the name of the Lord Jesus."[13] The reason is that the Son must abide by the strict justice of God (the legalistic framework again!), so if appeal is made

---

[12]See my chapter on the Virgin Mary in *The Faith: Understanding Orthodox Christianity* (Salisbury, MA: Regina Orthodox Press, 1997), pp. 115-126.

[13]Quoted in Graef, Part One, p. 216.

through Mary, He sees her merit, not the lack of merit in the supplicant.[14]

In the late fourteenth century Bridget, a Franciscan nun, supported the doctrine of the Immaculate Conception with the claim of "revelations" from the Virgin herself. According to Bridget, the Virgin shortens the life of sinners so their sufferings in hell will be less. She also said, in Mary's voice, "As Adam and Eve sold the world for one apple, so my Son and I have redeemed the world as it were with one heart (*Revelationes*, I, 35)." She even went so far as to call Mary *Salvatrix*.[15]

Such language dangerously blurs the distinction between creature and Creator. It leads, inevitably, to two further doctrines, the doctrine of the Assumption—dogmatized in 1950—and the idea of Mary as

[14]Of course, the Orthodox Church believes very strongly in the intercessions of the Mother of God. However, the idea, so common in Western piety, that the Virgin Mary saves man from the just anger of her Son is absurd. As said above (Chapter 3), God does not "get angry." Our Lord Jesus Christ does not need His mother to calm Him down. Graef notes: "Thus the West continued the line that had begun with the Greek prayer *Sub tuum praesidium* in the third or fourth century—which, incidentally, Eadmer echoes several times (e.g., in *Tractatus XL*; where Mary is called the 'sigulare praesidium omnium ad te confugientium', the 'unique help of all who fly to you'), but in a way which presents the Mother of God more and more as an all-but-independent power ruling the whole world by the side of her Son, on whom she continues to exercise her maternal authority." Part One, p. 221.

[15]Graef. Part one, p. 309.

Coredemptrix, which many Roman Catholics are urging Pope John Paul II to declare as a dogma.

The Orthodox Church certainly believes that the body of the Mother of God was assumed into heaven. This is celebrated liturgically at the Feast of the Dormition (Falling Asleep) of the Theotokos on August 15. However, the papal bull defining the dogma of the Assumption (*Munificentissimus Deus*) is deliberately vague about whether or not she actually died: "that the immaculate Mother of God, Mary ever Virgin, when the course of her earthly life was run, was assumed in body and soul to heavenly glory."[16]

Frederick Holweck, in the encyclopedia article cited above, states unequivocally that while Mary was exempt from original sin, she was not exempt from the temporal penalties of Adam's sin, such as sickness and death. This, however, makes no sense whatsoever. If the Virgin is exempt from the guilt of Adam's sin and possesses the original justice, then it would be *unjust* for her to be subject to the temporal penalty of sin. Hence the vagueness of the definition. Furthermore, even if she did die, could it not be considered in someway a *voluntary* acceptance of death, parallel to that of her Son?[17]

---

[16]Graef calls it "studiously vague." Part Two, p. 147.

[17]The liturgical celebration of the Falling Asleep of the Virgin is fairly late, and material on the subject before the fifth century is scant and contradictory. Some, such as Epiphanius of Cyprus claimed not to know what happened to her. By the sixth century, however, the tradition had become much more settled. The major sources clearly indicated that she died, and her body was assumed into heaven after her burial. For an excellent introduction to the

This brings us to the concept of Mary as Coredemptrix. There is currently a movement — though the idea is by no means new — to have Pope John Paul II declare the Virgin Mary to be "Coredemptrix, Mediatrix of all Graces, and Advocate of the People of God."[18] According to supporters, Mary, through her suffering at the foot of the Cross, somehow participated with Christ, indeed, *helped* Him in His objective act of the redemption of mankind.

All Christians are called to be co-sufferers with Christ. St. Paul even speaks of making up in his body that which was lacking in the suffering of Christ (Col. 1:24). This, however, is not what is meant by calling Mary Coredemptrix. Nor does the doctrine mean that Mary played a unique role in the history of salvation by giving flesh to the Word of God. Rather, Mary's suffering, in a unique way, not shared by other Christian, somehow cooperates with the suffering of Christ in bringing about the redemption of man.

If we remove this idea from the legalistic framework of Roman Catholic soteriology and place it in the framework of Orthodox soteriology, then its absurdity becomes apparent. Certainly, Mary is man's "Yes" to God. By her *fiat* she, in her own person, receives the Creator into the world. Yet only God could recapitulate humanity within Himself. Only God could

subject see Brian E. Dailey, S.J., *On the Dormition of Mary: Early Patristic Homilies* (Crestwood, NY: SVS Press, 1998.

[18]In the United States, the movement is being led by Prof. Mark Miravalle of the Franciscan University of Steubenville, International president of Vox Populi Mariae Mediatrici.

destroy the power of death, by filling it with His immortal life. What could the Virgin possibly contribute to that, except for contributing the flesh He assumed?[19]

The Orthodox venerate the Mother of God as "more honorable than the cherubim and more glorious beyond compare than the seraphim." However, the Mother of God did not shed her blood for the life of the world; she did not give her life a ransom for many; she did not empty Hades of its captives; she did not become the firstfruits of them that slept; she will not come again to judge the living and the dead. Calling Mary Coredemptrix, therefore, is not simply wrong, it is blasphemous and heretical.

The Power of Popular Piety

There is no question that, historically, the dogma of the Immaculate Conception was controversial. Likewise, the concept of Mary as Coredemptrix is controversial. What then is the motivation for defining these ideas as official dogmas of the Church? The answer, quite simply, is popular piety. This is

[19]Supporters of this idea cite the attribution of the title "New Eve" to Mary by early Fathers such as Irenaeus as proof of the idea's antiquity. This, however, is an utterly dishonest use of the Fathers. For Irenaeus, as for the other Fathers of the early Church, Mary is the New Eve because her "Yes" is the answer to Eve's "No." Her obedience is the answer to Eve's disobedience. It has nothing whatsoever to do with the notion that her emotional sufferings at the foot of the Cross added to or even participated in the act of redemption.

manifested in two ways. First, there is the desire to glorify the Mother of God as much as possible and to define Her role in salvation as fully as possible. Second, one cannot underestimate the impact that various Marian apparitions have had.

The Marian doctrines of the Immaculate Conception and the Assumption, as well as the would-be doctrine of Coredemptrix, are the product of a desire, no doubt pious, to give the Mother of God as much glory as possible. Peter of Candia (later Pope Alexander V) said of the Immaculate Conception, "I would rather err by an excess of praise than of blame."[20] In other words, it is better to say too much than too little. The letter of petition to Pope John Paul II urging him to define the doctrine of Coredemptrix states, "It is our belief that such a definition will bring to light the whole truth about Mary, Daughter of the Father, Mother of the Son, Spouse of the Spirit and Mother of the Church." Thus, there is a desire to define the "whole truth" about Mary.

This principle, which seems to run implicitly throughout most "developments of doctrine" in the Roman Catholic Church, is patently at variance with the way the early Church approached the question of dogma. All early conciliar definitions of dogma were the response to specific heresies. The Church defined the doctrine of the Trinity in response to Arianism and Eunomianism, and even then the Church never pretended to define the "whole truth" about the

---

[20]Graef, Part One, p. 311.

THE MOTHER OF GOD

mystery of the Trinity. Similarly, the Christological definitions of the later councils were occasioned by the heresies of Nestorianism, Monophysitism, Monotheletism, and Iconoclasm. Nowhere did the Fathers of these councils claim to have exhausted the "whole truth" about the mystery of the Incarnation. These definitions *never ever* presumed to explain these mysteries, but to *exclude* false opinions. They were not so much positive statements as negative ones.

The definition of the Virgin Mary as Theotokos (Birthgiver of God) is particularly instructive here. The Council of Ephesus (425) was called to deal with the teaching of Patriarch Nestorius of Constantinople. He taught that Mary was not the Mother of God, but of the man Jesus, thereby implying two subjects in the person of Christ: the Son of God and the man, Jesus. The dogmatic definition of Mary as Mother of God was, therefore, made to ensure a proper understanding of *Christ*.

Now, what heresy concerning the nature of God, Christ, or man's salvation necessitated the bull defining the Immaculate Confession in 1854, or the promulgation of the Assumption in 1950?[21] Furthermore, what could possibly necessitate the promulgation

[21]This explains the lukewarm reception to the promulgation of the Assumption by the Orthodox. Even though the Orthodox Church believes the Virgin was assumed into heaven after her death, this pious belief is not *required* by dogma. As Fr. Michael Pomazansky states, "The Church, accepting the tradition of the ascension of the body of the Mother of God, has not regarded and does not regard this pious tradition as one of the fundamental truths or dogmas of the Christian faith" (p. 195).

of Mary as Coredemptrix other than an arrogant and delusional desire to define the "whole truth" about the Mother of God?

Fr. John Meyendorff was fond of saying that Orthodoxy is the only religion that does not require one to believe anything that is not true.[22] This may seem like a rather backhanded compliment, but it contains a profound truth. The Orthodox Church only dogmatizes that which is *essential* to man's salvation. The Church does not dogmatize matters of opinion (*theologoumena*).

The Roman Catholic Church, on the other hand, has demonstrated a penchant for doing just that. Why do popes do this? Because they *can*. It seems almost as if popular piety gives the Roman pontiffs the excuse they need to exercise their power to infallibly define new dogmas.

The influence of popular piety is clearly seen in the impact Marian apparitions have had on the development of these doctrines. Bridget had visions of the Mother of God, who confirmed the doctrine of the Immaculate Conception. Four years after the promulgation of the dogma, Bernadette of Lourdes saw visions of a small lady who told her, "I am the Immaculate Conception."[23] Numerous appearances of the Virgin have confirmed that she is the Coredemptrix.

Two points need to be made at this juncture. First of all, in the Orthodox tradition, stories of visions and appearances are rare. On the whole, the spiritual

[22]I doubt if this was original to Fr. Meyendorff. I have heard it attributed to several people, including Fr. Georges Florovsky.
[23]Pelikan, *Mary*, p. 199.

literature of the Church counsels Christians to be very wary of such visions. Indeed, there are numerous stories of monks and nuns being deceived by visions of "angels." At any rate, even if a vision can be accepted as authentic—and this is rare—visions are certainly no basis for defining dogma.

Second, a great many of these visions (Bernadette, Fatima, Medjugorja) occurred to a child or children. The children go into a trance-like state, see a vision of the Mother of God, and are given messages, including "secrets." Aside from the fact that children are highly susceptible to suggestion, and can hardly be relied upon as dependable witnesses, such phenomena run counter to the experiences of the Saints in the Orthodox Church. Those in the Church who *have* been given visions of the Mother of God or the Saints are usually experienced, ascetics. That is, persons who had purified themselves through prayer and ascetical struggle.

Furthermore, I know of no precedents in Church history for the Mother of God giving "secrets." The whole thing sounds more like Freemasonry than Christian spirituality. Such widespread acceptance of visions can only occur where there is a tremendous lack of spiritual discernment.

Fatima

Before I close out this chapter, I want to say a few words about the Fatima "prophecies," primarily because they bear directly upon Orthodox-Roman

Catholic Relations.[24] In 1917 a young Portuguese girl named Lucia and two cousins began to have visions of the Virgin. At one point the Virgin told Lucia that World War I would end on October 13. In point of fact, it did not end for thirteen more months.[25] Despite this false prophecy — a universally recognized sign of a false prophet — millions of Roman Catholics, among them Popes Pius XI, Pius XII, and John Paul II, have accepted the visions as genuine.

In addition to the Virgin's incorrect prediction, she gave Lucia a series of three "secrets." The third secret is in the possession of the Vatican and has not been publicly revealed, although it is reported that Pope John Paul II has seen it. The second secret is the one that concerns us here. The Virgin told Lucia that if the pope would consecrate Russia to her Immaculate Heart, then she would promise unconditionally the conversion of Russia.[26] This would usher in a period of world peace.

First of all, I simply cannot refrain from commenting about this bizarre Roman Catholic fixation with body parts, be it the Sorrowful and/or Immaculate Heart of Mary or the Sacred Heart of Christ. Such piety is utterly foreign to the Orthodox consciousness.

[24]For a general introduction, see Graef, Part Two, pp. 136-140. While careful not to dismiss these vision stories, Graef shows a tremendous degree of restraint in discussing them. It is clear that she takes them with a grain of salt.

[25]Graef, p. 139.

[26]Graef writes, "It is hard to see why a formal act of consecration should have such a tremendous effect; as Fr. Martindale pointed out, 'the conversion of the world was not unconditionally attached to Calvary itself.' p. 140.

Second, the unconditional promise of the conversion of Russia raises a red flag for the Orthodox. Pope Pius XII consecrated Russia to the Immaculate Heart in 1952.[27] Furthermore, Pope John Paul II has declared his belief in the visions. What can this mean other than that Rome expects the Orthodox country of Russia to *convert* to Roman Catholicism? Furthermore, it is no secret that the Fatima visions lie behind a great deal of the movement for missionary activity in Russia. So much for the notion that Rome only desires a "reunion of Churches"! Rome desires not reunion, but subjugation.

Third, the promise of world peace should be enough to tip anyone off that these "prophecies" are not from the Mother of God, but the Father of Lies. According to the Scriptures, the end of the age will come with *wars and rumors of wars* (Mat. 24:6). To be sure, a (brief) period of worldwide peace will be ushered in, but not by the Mother of God, rather by the Antichrist.

In short, the Fatima "prophecies" are demonic delusions. That tens of thousands, if not millions, of Roman Catholics (including several popes) have been deceived by this is a testimony that the Spirit of

[27]Graef, Part Two, p. 140. However, an internet website devoted to the Fatima cult (www.fatima.org—I cite this even though I have an old fashioned prejudice against citing the internet in formal writing) does not mention this consecration and states that the consecration of Russia has yet to take place. According to the website, the Virgin requires that *all* the world's bishops join the pope.

Discernment has left the Roman Church. But how could it be otherwise? For it was the Roman Catholic Church that subordinated and marginalized the Holy Spirit with the doctrine of the *Filioque*. It was the Roman Church that defined the energies of the Spirit[28] as created effects, thereby robbing man of a direct participation in God, limiting him to an external, legalistic understanding of salvation, and denying him the possibility of deification. It was the Roman Church that eliminated the need for the Spirit of Unity within the Church by modeling her organization after that of the Roman Empire, creating a universal, political organization, headed by a single, infallible monarch. Given this, the excesses of Marian devotion seem almost inevitable.

[28]Cf. the "Seven Spirits of God" from Rev. 4:5.

A Note for Evangelicals Considering Rome

> We preserve the Doctrine of the Lord uncor-
> rupted, and firmly adhere to the Faith He deliv-
> ered to us, and keep it free from blemish and
> diminution, as a Royal Treasure, and a monu-
> ment of great price, neither adding anything,
> nor taking anything from it (Eastern Patriarchs
> to the English Non-Jurors, 1718).

Sooner or later, Protestants who are serious about their faith—serious about what it means to be a Christian and to be a member of "the Church"—begin to look beyond the borders of their limited denominational existence for a more profound spirituality, a God-centered experience of worship, and a concrete sense of belonging to an historical Christian community. In the 1970's this searching gave rise to a movement called "Catholic Evangelicalism." This was a movement among Evangelicals to recover their lost "catholic" heritage while remaining within their Protestant denominations.[1]

---

[1]Cf. Donald G. Bloesch, *The Future of Evangelical Christianity: A Call for Unity Amid Diversity* (Garden City: Doubleday & Co., 1983), pp. 48-52.

This movement reached a high point with a gathering of 46 Evangelical leaders in 1977. The resulting "Chicago Call" was a challenge to the Evangelical world to take the past seriously and to recover much of traditional Christian life that had been "thrown out with the bath water" during the Reformation.[2] Interestingly, however, several of the "high profile" signers of the Chicago Call discovered that they could not recover their "catholic roots" while remaining Protestant. Some became Orthodox and some, Thomas Howard in particular, became Roman Catholic.[3]

While Evangelical voices such as *Christianity Today* tried to pass these conversions off as romantic flights of fancy, the number of conversions continues to increase.[4] More recently, two prominent American Lutherans have converted: (now Father) Richard John Neuhaus, author of *The Naked Public Square*, became a Roman

[2]The text of the Chicago Call may be found in Robert Webber, *Common Roots: A Call to Evangelical Maturity* (Grand Rapids: Zondervan, 1978), pp. 251-256.

[3]Robert Webber and Donald Bloesch are somewhat conspicuous in that they have steadfastly remained in their Protestant denominations — denominations that are among the most liberal in America. Webber is a member of the Episcopal Church and, as far as I know, Bloesch remains a member of the United Church of Christ.

[4]For an account of eighteen Protestant pastors who converted to Orthodoxy see Peter Gillquist, Ed. *Coming Home: Why Protestant Clergy are Becoming Orthodox* (Ben Lomond, CA: Conciliar Press, 1992). Perhaps the most visible Evangelical to convert was Frank Schaeffer, son of the late theologian Francis Schaeffer. See his *Dancing Alone: The Quest for Orthodox Faith in the Age of False Religion* (Brookline, MA: Holy Cross Orthodox Press, 1994).

Catholic, and Yale historian Jaroslav Pelikan became Orthodox.[5]

In short, there has been a definite movement, particularly among clergy and intellectuals, from Protestantism toward what may be termed the catholic tradition. The question that faces Protestants looking for the catholic tradition, however, is which Church embodies it: the Roman Catholic Church or the Orthodox Church?

In order to help Evangelicals make a reasoned evaluation of these rival claims, it would be beneficial to examine the reasons why some Evangelicals choose Roman Catholicism over Orthodoxy. To this end, let us turn our attention to the story of Scott and Kimberly Hahn, as recounted in their book *Rome Sweet Home: Our Journey to Catholicism.*[6] Scott, a young Presbyterian minister, and his wife could hardly have started out more anti-Catholic. Since their conversions, however, they have become well-known Catholic apologists.

In particular, I want to focus on Scott's consideration — and rejection — of Orthodoxy. It takes him all of two paragraphs (out of 182 pages) to explain this, so I will reproduce the passage in full:

> So I started looking into Orthodoxy. I met with Peter Gilquist, an evangelical convert to Antiochene Orthodoxy, to hear why he chose Orthodoxy over Rome. His reasons reinforced my sense that Prot-

[5]Pelikan was received into the Orthodox Church on March 25, 1998 (The Feast of the Annunciation) at St. Vladimir's Orthodox Theological Seminary in New York.

[6]San Francisco: Ignatius Press, 1993.

estantism was wrong; but I also thought that his defense of Orthodoxy over Catholicism was unsatisfying and superficial. Upon closer examination, I found the various Orthodox churches to be hopelessly divided among themselves, similar to the Protestants, except that the Orthodox were split along the lines of ethnic nationalisms; there were Orthodox bodies that called themselves Greek, Russian, Ruthenian, Rumanian, Bulgarian, Hungarian, Serbian and so on. They have coexisted for centuries, but more like a family of brothers who have lost their father.

Further study led me to conclude that Orthodoxy was wonderful for its liturgy and tradition but stagnant in theology. In addition, I became convinced that it was mistaken in doctrine, having rejected certain teachings of Scripture and the Catholic Church, especially the *filioque* clause ("and the Son") that had been added to the Nicene Creed. In addition, their rejection of the Pope as head of the Church seemed to be based on imperial politics, more than on any serious theological grounds. This helped me to understand why, throughout their history, Orthodox Christians have tended to exalt the Emperor and the State over the Bishop and the Church (otherwise known as "Caesaropapism"). It occurred to me that Russia had been reaping the consequences of this Orthodox outlook throughout the twentieth century.

While Hahn's investigation of Orthodoxy must have been more involved than he describes in this passage, it is clear that he did not put a great amount of effort into it. His reasons for choosing Roman Catholicism over Orthodoxy sound as if they came directly from a 19th century anti-Orthodox tract.

Orthodoxy and Ethnicism

Let us begin with his meeting with *Father* Peter Gillquist.[7] Now, I have known   Fr. Peter for many years, and have the greatest personal admiration and respect for him. However, Fr. Peter himself would never claim to be a theologian or a scholar. I am not surprised, therefore, that Hahn found Fr. Peter's thoughts on Roman Catholicism less than profound. He would have been better served by talking with people who have a first hand knowledge of Roman Catholicism, such as Fr. Alexey Young[8] or Fr. Theodore Pulcini.[9]

Furthermore, Fr. Peter is not a convert to "Antiochene Orthodoxy." There is simply no such thing. Fr. Peter serves in the American archdiocese of the Patriarchate of Antioch. Orthodoxy, however, is Orthodoxy, whether it is practiced among Syrians, Russians, Greeks, or Americans. The claim that "the various Orthodox churches [are] hopelessly divided among themselves, similar to the Protestants, except that the Orthodox were split along the lines of ethnic nationalisms" is

[7]Aside from the fact that Hahn fails to give Fr. Peter proper respect by using his ecclesiastical title, Hahn also misspells his name.

[8]See Alexey Young, *The Rush to Embrace* (Richfield Springs, NY: Nikodemos Orthodox Publication Society, 1996).

[9]Fr. Theodore has a small booklet entitled, *Orthodoxy and Catholicism: What are the Differences?* (Ben Lomond, CA: Conciliar Press, 1995).

patently absurd. It is the kind of cliché that is often trot-
ted out by Protestants and Roman Catholics alike who
are too lazy to undertake a serious investigation of the
matter.

To begin with, the division of the Orthodox world
into various, self-governing "national Churches" has
more to do with the Western European phenomenon of
nationalism and the subsequent interference of Western
powers (Great Britain, in particular) in the internal affairs of the Balkan nations than it does with the internal
logic of Orthodoxy.[10] While nationalism has been and
remains a problem for Orthodoxy, it is in no way of the
essence of Orthodoxy. Indeed, in 1872 the Orthodox
Church formally condemned as a heresy the theory that
the Church should be organized according to ethnic

---

[10]Fr. John Meyendorff observes: "In Greece and in the other
Balkan countries of Bulgaria, Serbia and Romania, nationalism was
generally promoted by a western-trained and western-oriented
secularized *intelligentsia* which had no real interest in Orthodoxy
and the Church except as a useful tool for achieving secular na-
tionalistic goals." "Ecclesiastical Regionalism: Structures of Communion or Cover for Separatism," originally published in *St. Vladimir's Theological Quarterly* 24 (1980), pp. 155-168. Reprinted in
Meyendorff, *The Byzantine Legacy in the Orthodox Church*, pp. 217-
233 (226). It should be noted that this essay was originally written
for an ecumenical colloquium and is far from being "anti-western."
The reader should be aware, however, that Fr. John's criticism of
modern Orthodox regionalism and his expressed openness to the
concept of Roman primacy in this article is part of an intellectual
dialogue and can in no way be interpreted as a denial of the basic
tenets of Orthodox ecclesiology, which clearly rule out concepts
such as universal ordinary jurisdiction. See our discussion of primacy below in Chapter 4.

make-up rather than according to territorial dioceses (*phyletism*).[11]

What Hahn fails to mention here is that each of these "national Churches" professes one and the same Orthodox Faith, observes one and the same liturgical life (albeit in different languages and local customs), and maintains full eucharistic communion with the others.[12] The fact that they do not all answer to a single

---

[11]See Meyendorff, "Ecclesiastical Regionalism," p. 228.

[12]There are two primary exceptions to this worldwide Orthodox unity. The first involves the Church calendar. In 1923, Ecumenical Patriarch Meletios Metaxakis (whose career was "colorful" to say the least, and the legitimacy of whose election is highly questionable) abandoned the traditional Orthodox (Julian) calendar and adopted the Gregorian calendar. Leaving aside the fact that such a calendar change had been condemned by previous Orthodox synods, the action was undertaken without the universal consent of the other Orthodox Churches—a *de facto* denial of the conciliar structure of the Church. It was, to put it bluntly, the result of papal pretensions on the part of the patriarch. The calendar change was adopted by several (but not all) local Churches, prompting schisms in Greece, Romania, and Bulgaria that have lasted to the present day. The calendar change—and I am a member of a local Church that uses the new, Gregorian calendar—was an unalloyed evil and a curse for the Church. It would have never happened, however, had the conciliar nature of the Church not been utterly disregarded. For a decidedly unsympathetic treatment of Patriarch Melitios and the calendar change see Bishop Photius of Triaditsa, "The 70th Anniversary of the Pan-Orthodox Congress in Constantinople" in *the Orthodox Church Calendar: In Defense of the Julian Calendar* (Jordanville, NY: Holy Trinity Monastery, 1996), pp. 5-29. The second exception to Orthodox unity is a direct result of the Russian Revolution: the division between the Church of Russia (Moscow Patriarchate) and the Russian Church Abroad (a.k.a. the "Synod"). With the demise of the Soviet Union, however, tentative efforts

bishop in a foreign country in no way means that they are not truly united in one, Catholic Church. To liken the different local Churches to different Protestant denominations is ludicrous.

Now it is certainly true that the presence of multiple, overlapping jurisdictions in America is a great problem and a cause for scandal. However, it must be noted that this sad situation is the result of particular historical circumstances well beyond the power of anyone to control. Before the Russian Revolution of 1917, North America was *de facto* the missionary territory of the Russian Church. Aside from the dominant presence of the Orthodox Church in Alaska (formerly Russian territory), Orthodox missionaries moved south along the West Coast during the 19th century.[13]

When Orthodox from the Mediterranean and Eastern Europe began to arrive in America, most went under the care of the existing Russian Church structure. The first Syrian bishop in America, Rafael Hawaweeny, was actually a bishop of the Russian Orthodox Church.

---

have begun to heal this breach. Lest Roman Catholics get too smug in observing these intra-Orthodox problems, however, we should point out that the entire Reformation, with its thousands of resulting denominations, started out as a schism within the Roman Church. Furthermore, there exist other bodies that claim to represent true Roman Catholicism, notably the Old Catholic Church of Utrecht and the Polish National Catholic Church.

[13]For the history of the Alaskan mission as well as a general treatment of Orthodox missiology, see the two excellent studies by Fr. Michael Oleksa: *Alaskan Missionary Spirituality* (New York: Paulist Press, 1987) and *Orthodox Alaska: A Theology of Mission* (Crestwood, NY: SVS Press, 1992).

While many Greek communities maintained a separate existence, bringing priests over from Greece, their requests for bishops were always denied, because there were already Orthodox bishops here, and the Churches of Greece and Constantinople were not willing to establish a parallel hierarchy.

The Russian Revolution, however, created problems not only for the Church in Russia, but for the Church in America as well. In the ensuing chaos, multiple Orthodox jurisdictions were established as the individual immigrant communities appealed to their mother Churches for help. As time went by, people got used to this unusual arrangement. Thus, for example, you can find in a single city a "Greek," a "Russian," and a "Serbian" Orthodox Church.

It must be noted here that no one today considers this situation to be normal or even acceptable. All Orthodox jurisdictions in this country are aware of the fact that the situation is "uncanonical." Of course, if Orthodoxy had a universal pope, he could "fix" the situation by *fiat*. Then again, he could also "infallibly" define strange doctrines and compel everyone to assent to them under pain of excommunication. A certain degree of disorganization is the price the Church pays for not succumbing to the temptations of worldly success and order.

Caesaropapism

There have, of course, been times when the Church was more or less forced into a more "efficient" mode of operation by secular powers, and the Church suffered dearly for such intrusions. That is what makes Hahn's comments about caesaropapism so utterly galling. To suggest that the Orthodox Church accepted a state of affairs whereby the emperor decided Church policy and that this is in contrast to the way things worked in the West, where Rome claimed supremacy over the temporal powers, displays an appalling ignorance of history.

To begin with, Orthodox canon law specifically forbids state interference in the internal workings of the Church. That does not mean that emperors did not try to interfere in the Church's business—most tried, and some were more successful than others. It does mean, however, that the Church never accepted this as a normal state of affairs. Indeed, the Church calendar is filled with saints who suffered mightily for their refusal to go along with imperial policy.[14]

There is a great irony here. By far the greatest impetus for reunion with Rome prior to the fall of Constantinople came from *imperial* political motives. It was in the interest of the emperor to have communion restored

[14]"Caesaropapism, however, never became an accepted principle in Byzantium. Innumerable heroes of the faith were constantly exalted precisely because they had opposed heretical emperors; hymns sung in church praised Basil for having disobeyed Valens, Maximus for his martyrdom under Constans, and numerous monks for having opposed the iconoclastic emperors in the eighth century. These liturgical praises alone were sufficient to safeguard the principle that the emperor was to preserve, not to define, the Christian faith." John Meyendorff, *Byzantine Theology: Historical Trends and Doctrinal Themes* (New York: Fordham University Press, 1983), p. 6.

between the Orthodox and the Church of Rome because of the political advantages it would bring.[15] The so-called "union councils" of Lyons (1274) and Florence (1439) were both promoted by the emperor, and both rejected by the body of the Orthodox faithful. Were Hahn's views of caesaropapism correct, then the Church would have dutifully obeyed imperial policy, and Rome and Orthodoxy would be in communion now![16]

The fact is, the only place in the Orthodox world where caesaropapism was ever close to being an ac-

---

[15]Remember that Constantinople was facing overwhelming odds in defending herself against the Moslems.

[16]"From the thirteenth century on, all discussions between the popes and emperors regarding reunion took place in an atmosphere dominated more by political than by religious considerations, the Byzantine Church itself remaining largely outside the picture. Moreover, those discussions showed that the West harbored completely false ideas about the existence of Byzantine caesaropapism and thought that it was sufficient to win over the emperor to gain the allegiance of the whole Church. It was with this in mind that the popes encouraged the personal conversion of the Emperor John V in 1369. Even today the view is quite common that the Byzantine 'schism' had its roots in caesaropapism; nevertheless it is a fact that from the eleventh century the emperors were almost consistently in favor of reunion with Rome because of the undoubted political advantages to be derived from it, and they tried to bring reunion about at all costs, even by the use of brute force. Equally consistently, since the time of Michael Caerularius, the patriarchs, or most of them at any rate, opposed their efforts in the name of the true faith. By relying so much on the emperors to bring about reunion, the popes were relying, actually, on a caesaropapism which did not in fact exist." Meyendorff, *Orthodox Church*, pp. 59-60.

cepted reality was in Russia, subsequent to the reforms of Peter "the Great." Peter abolished the office of patriarch, installed his own government *oberprocurator* for religious affairs to oversee the Holy Synod, and effectively made the Church a department of state. There is no doubt that this severely weakened the Church and contributed to Her inability to successfully counter the communist Revolution.[17] What non-Orthodox historians invariably omit, however, is the fact that the Petrine reforms were based on church-state relations Peter had observed in the German and Scandinavian principalities. Thus, Petrine Russia's caesaropapism was the direct result of Western, non-Orthodox influences.[18]

[17]The Patriarchate was re-established at an All-Russian council literally during the October Revolution. Unfortunately, the reforms came too late to stop the communist take over of the government. Interestingly, the newly elected patriarch, St. Tikhon, had been the Archbishop of New York, overseeing the American mission before his election. For an account of the reform movement prior to the Revolution, see James W. Cunningham, *A Vanquished Hope: The Movement for Church Renewal in Russia, 1905-1906* (Crestwood, NY: SVS Press, 1981).

[18]Cf. Fr. Georges Florovsky, *Ways of Russian Theology*, Part One; Vol. 5 in *The Collected Works of Georges Florovsky*, Tr. by Robert Nichols (Belmont, MA: Nordland, 1979). "Peter wished to organize church administration in Russia just as Protestant countries ordered it. Such a reorganization did not just correspond to his own estimation of his authority or merely follow from the logic of his general conception of state authority or the 'monarch's will.' It also conformed to his personal religious perception or opinion. Peter's outlook was wholly that of a man of the Reformation world, even if he retained in his personal life an unexpectedly large number of habits and impulses belonging to the Muscovite past" (pp.117-118). "The 'Reformation' remained an act of secular coercion, compelling

Hahn's comment that the sufferings of the Russian Church under the Soviet regime were the fruit of an "Orthodox outlook" is as stupid as it is insulting.

Before we leave the subject of church-state relations, let us consider the following:

> It would be impossible for him to be corrupted by anyone, for he is a catholic in faith, a king in power, a pontiff in preaching, a judge in equity, a philosopher in liberal studies, a model in morals.[19]

A panegyric to a Roman emperor written by a sycophantic Orthodox bishop? Hardly. This particular tribute was written by Alcuin in honor of Charlemagne, the Frankish usurper crowned "Holy Roman Emperor" by Pope Leo III in 800.

The crowning of Charlemagne is often cited as an example of papal supremacy over temporal powers. In reality, however, the Church in Western Europe became part of the Germanic feudal system, with clergy appointed and "invested" by secular rulers. Simony became a matter of course. This situation did not change until the Gregorian Reforms of the eleventh century. Even then, however, claims of papal supremacy over

the body of the church to wither but finding no sympathetic response in the depths of the church's consciousness" (p. 120). And again: "The church's mind and conscience never became accustomed to, accepted, or acknowledged this actual 'caesaropapism,' although individual churchmen and leaders frequently with inspiration submitted to it. The mystical fullness of the church remained unharmed" (p. 121).

[19]Quoted in Pelikan, *Growth*, pp. 51-52.

matters temporal did not always match reality. Pelikan observes:

> What the history books describe as the "investiture controversy" was not merely the church's defense of its own right to select and install its bishops. It was also the state's defense against the claims of the church. The pope claimed the right to depose the emperor, and in the investiture controversy he tried to do just that. Repeatedly pope and emperor clashed over the limits of their respective jurisdictions. The zenith of papal power under Pope Innocent III (d. 1216) was followed less than a century later by the exile of the pope in Avignon and by the humiliating history of the papacy in the fourteenth and fifteenth centuries. Through it all the pope claimed authority over the state as well as the church, but conditions within the church seemed to many to prove that he could not rule even the church.[20]

Clearly, Hahn's reading of church history is both selective and inaccurate. Ever since the time Jesus was presented with a Roman coin and asked about taxation, Christians have been trying to come to terms with the proper relationship between Church and state. No one—in the East or in the West—was able to come up with a perfect solution. Indeed, a perfect solution is not

[20]Jaroslav Pelikan, *The Riddle of Roman Catholicism*, p. 44. At least one Roman Catholic writer cites the Church's involvement with secular rule as a tragedy: "But from the time the popes entered the temporal arena, heavy and irremovable chains were forged around their churchly kingdom." Malachi Martin, *The Decline and Fall of the Roman Church* (NY: Putnam, 1981), p.14.

possible in this world, for the Reign of God is *not of this world* (Jn. 18:36).[21]

Theology

With Hahn's comment concerning Orthodox theology, he moves from the absurd to the surreal: "Further study led me to conclude that Orthodoxy was wonderful for its liturgy and tradition but stagnant in theology." If the alternative to being "stagnant" means changing the creed (the *Filioque*), worrying about going to a non-existent place (purgatory), paying money to stay out of said non-existent place (indulgences), turning the Virgin Mary into some sort of super-human (an immaculately conceived Coredemptrix), and making the bishop of one city into an infallible, universal potentate with both spiritual and political sovereignty, then the Orthodox will gladly stay stagnant.

The really amusing thing about Hahn's comment is that it sounds like something one would expect to hear from the ultra-liberal Episcopal bishop John Spong—complete with a patronizing reference to Orthodoxy's "wonderful" liturgy. The "development of doctrine" is the excuse used by Roman Catholics to justify every change in doctrine from the *Filioque* to papal infallibility. Yet, liberals also believe that their modernizations are justified by the notion of progress. In the final analysis, what is the real difference between the "improvements" of Christianity made by the Roman

[21]The Kingdom of God (ἡ βασιλεία τοῦ Θεοῦ) is more properly rendered as the Reign of God.

Catholic Church and the "improvements" wrought by liberals such as Spong? [22]

The similarities between a conservative Roman Catholic such as Hahn and a liberal Protestant such as Spong are more than superficial. In his classic introduction to Orthodoxy, Bishop Kallistos Ware quotes the nineteenth-century Russian theologian Alexis Khomiakov:

> All Protestants are Crypto-Papists. To use the concise language of algebra, all the West knows but one datum a; whether it be preceded by the positive sign +, as with the Romanists, or with the negative -, as with the Protestants, the a remains the same. [23]

Thus, Roman Catholicism and Protestantism are but two sides of the same coin. They may present different faces, but the underlying substance is the same.

This explains why many conservative Protestants are attracted to Rome. Allegiance to Rome allows them to overcome the inherent inconsistencies in Protestant-

---

[22]Hahn has added his name to the list of Roman Catholics petitioning the pope to declare the Virgin Mary as "Coredemptrix." He, and another professor from the Franciscan University at Steubenville, have prepared a three part audio series on the doctrine. According to the advertisement for the tape: "Scott explains how Mary was a stumbling block in his conversion, and why he was, as a new Catholic, reluctant to support a new Marian dogma. He then shows how this dogma captures Mary's vital importance, especially as the new millennium draws near, which Pope John Paul II anticipates will be a 'new springtime' for the Church." If the new millennium demands new dogmas, might it just as well demand a new code of morality?

[23]Timothy (Kallistos) Ware, *The Orthodox Church*, p. 9.

ism without having to abandon the basic presupposition of Protestantism, namely that Christianity is an ideology derived from a text.[24]

Sola Scriptura is patently illogical. The popular Protestant saying, "The Bible says it; that settles it" makes no sense because, strictly speaking, the Bible does not "say" anything. It is a text, and like all texts it must be interpreted. An infallible book is only useful if you have an infallible interpreter, which is where the pope comes in. Where two or three Protestants are gathered together, there you have four or five different interpretations of the Bible. With an infallible pope, however, you only have to deal with one interpretation—at a time, that is.[25] "The pope says it; that settles it."

We have already discussed why the Roman Catholic doctrine of the papacy is fundamentally incompatible with the Orthodox faith, so I shall not recover that ground here. However, I do want to stress the fundamental unity of Roman Catholicism and Protestantism. The Hahns did not really *convert* to anything; they merely exchanged one form of the same authoritarian, rationalistic religion for another.

Hahn and other Catholic apologists go to great pains to demonstrate that Catholicism (both those elements which are genuinely part of the catholic tradition

[24]I develop this idea in *The Way: What Every Protestant Should Know About the Orthodox Church* (Salisbury, MA: Regina Orthodox Press, 1998).

[25]Popes, have, of course disagreed with one another. This also assumes that there are no anti-popes, thus making it difficult to tell which is the real infallible pontiff.

and those which are peculiar to the Roman Catholic Church) are based on the Word of God, both in its written and its oral form. Even if a doctrine cannot claim an uninterrupted history back to the Apostles (i.e. the Immaculate Conception or papal infallibility), it can nonetheless be considered "scriptural" if it can be logically deduced from the Bible.[26] This theological method— deducing a doctrine from a text—is the common heritage of Catholics and Protestants alike, even those Protestants who consider themselves to be the most anti-Catholic.

At this point, allow me to reiterate that Orthodoxy is in no way *based* on the Bible. Nor is it *based* on or *derived* from a set of oral teachings running parallel to the Bible. The Orthodox Church is the living Body of Christ— the living experience in history of the union of mankind with God in the divine-human Person of the Only-Begotten. The Word of God is not a book, but a Person. The Prophets, both those of the Old Covenant and those of the New, are those who have seen and heard and touched the Word of Life.[27] The Divine Scriptures and the writings of the Saints are the written *witness* to this experience, but they are not the *source* of this experience.

Thus, true and false doctrines are not discerned by whether or not one can logically deduce them from the text of the Bible or the writings of a particular Church

[26]I am using *deduced* here in its general sense, rather than in the way it is used in formal logic. Most of these "deductions" are in fact *inductions*, for very few could claim to be logically *necessary*.
[27]Cf. 1 Jn. 1:1.

Father—one can "deduce" just about anything from the Bible, as Protestantism has demonstrated several thousand times over—but whether or not the purported doctrine constitutes a faithful *witness* to or *sign* of the communion between God and man that is experienced in the Church. Thus, Orthodoxy rejects Roman Catholic doctrines such as papal infallibility or purgatory, not because they cannot be "deduced" from this or that Bible verse or patristic citation, but because they make a lie out of the Church's experience of union with God in Christ. False doctrines are *false witnesses*. They derive from and lead toward *false Christs.*[28]

Evangelicals searching for the catholic tradition must understand that Orthodoxy is not simply an alternative ecclesiastical structure to the Roman Catholic Church. The Orthodox Church presents a fundamentally different approach to theology, because She possesses a fundamentally different experience of Christ and life in Him. To put it bluntly, She knows a different Christ from that of the Roman Catholic Church.

Final Considerations

I converted to Holy Orthodoxy because I saw in the theology and life of the Orthodox Church a pure wit-

---

[28]"Consequently, when the heretic lays hands on the 'traditional faith' he lays hands on the life of the faithful, their *raison d'être*. Heresy is at once blasphemy towards God and a curse for man. This is the reason why the entire organism and the spiritual health and sensitivity of Orthodoxy has from the beginning reacted against the destructive infection of heresies." Archimandrite Vasileios, *Hymn of Entry*, p. 21.

ness to the truth—the truth of my own being created in the image of God.[29] It was not a matter of subjecting myself to an external authority, but of recognizing and embracing the truth of reality itself.

There is no question that the Roman Catholic Church is larger and better organized than the Orthodox Church. There is no question that the current Roman liturgy is more "accessible" to modern Americans than the long, sung services of the Orthodox Church.[30] Nor can it be denied that Roman Catholicism is easier to grasp intellectually, being neatly set forth in a highly rationalistic system. None of this, however, makes Roman Catholicism *true*. Our Lord said, *"I am the Truth."* He did not say, "I am Efficiency and Convenience."

When I renounced Protestantism and embraced Holy Orthodoxy I implicitly renounced Roman Catholicism as well, for Roman Catholicism and Protestantism are truly two sides of the same coin. When I abandoned the heretical notion of *sola Scriptura*, I also abandoned the presupposition that Christianity is an ideology that can be derived from a text. When I relinquished my role as an infallible Protestant pope, interpreting the Bible according to my own lights, I also relinquished the fantasy that there could be another infallible pope.

To put it another way, I was not content to settle for Protestantism repackaged in sacramental garb. I was looking for a truly new vision of the Christian faith, and I found that new vision in Orthodoxy. Of course, what

[29]I discuss my conversion in detail in *The Way*.
[30]This is due in no small part to the continual "dumbing-down" of the Roman Mass since Vatican II.

was *new to me* was in fact the *oldest* expression of Christianity. Orthodoxy was the religion of the early Church—even in Rome—before the pope became an infallible sovereign, before purgatory became peopled with millions of souls trying "to work off" their sins, hoping that some of the "excess merits" of the Saints might fall their way.

If you want to know what life in the early Church was like, look at the Orthodox Church today. She still confesses the Nicene-Constantinopolitan Creed without changes, still baptizes by triple immersion[31], still keeps Wednesdays and Fridays as fasting days[32], still observes rather strict fasting rules for Lent and Advent[33], and still celebrates the Holy Liturgy in forms that are much the same as they were in the sixth century.[34]

In short, Orthodoxy is what Roman Catholicism *used* to be. If, however, you are looking for a "new and improved" version of Christianity, then whether you remain Protestant or become a Roman Catholic matters

[31]Roman Catholic children are lucky to get the tops of their heads wet. Where in the Gospels did our Lord enjoin His Disciples to "sprinkle all nations"?

[32]Even the famous practice of "fish on Fridays" has largely been abandoned by Roman Catholics, at least in the United States.

[33]By and large, fasting in the Roman Church has been reduced to "giving up something" for Lent.

[34]This is easily contrasted with the folk masses, mariachi masses, polka masses, and even clown masses that have become staples of the modern Roman Church since Vatican II. Indeed, contemporary Roman Catholic worship looks more and more like the baby-boomer friendly "seeker services" that have become so popular in the Protestant world.

little. Find a church or parish that meets your needs and fits your lifestyle, one where you are comfortable — a church with a gymnasium might be nice.

If, on the other hand, you are genuinely searching for an encounter with the living God, then forsake all thoughts of comfort or lifestyle. Seek the truth, and settle for nothing less. I can tell you that you will find the truth in the Orthodox Church. Here you will encounter God. Here you will find the guidance you need for the healing and salvation of your soul.

APPENDICES

Letter to the Patriarch of Constantinople

A letter of protest sent to Ecumenical Patriarch Bartholomeos by the Sacred Community of Mount Athos in regard to the "Balamand Agreement" of 1993.[1]

December 8, 1993

To His Most Divine All Holiness, the Ecumenical Patriarch, our Father and Master, Kyr. Bartholomew,

Most Holy Father and Master:

The union of the Churches or, to be precise, the union of the heterodox with our One, Holy, Catholic, and Apostolic Orthodox Church is desirable to us also so that the Lord's prayer may be fulfilled, . . . *that they may be one* (John 17:21). At any rate, we understand

---

[1]This letter originally appeared in Greek in *Orthodoxos Typos*, March 18, 1994, and has been translated into Russian, Serbian and English. This translation is by George S. Gabriel, editor of *The Ark*, where it first appeared in English (Num. 39-40, August 1994). For the full text of the Balamand Agreement see *Eastern Churches Journal*, vol. 1, No. 1.

[this] and await [the union] according to the Orthodox interpretation. As Professor John Romanides reminds us, "Christ prays here that His disciples and their disciples may, in this life, become one in the vision of His glory (which He has by nature from the Father) when they become members of His Body, the Church. . ."[2]

For this reason, whenever heterodox Christians visit us, to whom we extend love and hospitality in Christ, we are painfully aware that we stand apart in faith and, because of this, we are not able to have ecclesiastical communion.

Schism, the division between the Orthodox and the Non-Chalcedonians first and between the Orthodox and the Westerners later, truly amounts to a tragedy about which we must not become silent or complacent.

In this context, therefore, we appreciate efforts made with fear of God and in accordance with Orthodox Tradition that look to a union that cannot take place through the silencing or minimizing of Orthodox doctrines, or through toleration of the false doctrines of

[2]To complete the thought of the author we continue the passage here: "...which would be formed on Pentecost and whose members were to be illuminated and glorified in this life... This is how the Fathers understand this prayer... It is certainly not a prayer for the union of churches... which have not the slightest understanding of glorification (*theosis*) and how to arrive at it in this life." From a rebuttal to the Balamand Agreement by the renowned Orthodox theologian, Fr. John S. Romanides, Professor of Theology, St. John Damascene (Antiochian) Orthodox Theological School, Balamand, Lebanon; Professor Emeritus, University of Thessalonica, Greece; former Professor of Orthodox Theology, Holy Cross Greek Orthodox Theological School, Brookline, MA.

the heterodox, because it would not be a union in the Truth. And then in the end, it would not be accepted by the Church or blessed by God, because, according to the patristic saying, "A good thing is not good if it is not achieved in a good way."

On the contrary, it would bring about new schisms and new divisions and miseries to the already [dis]united[3] body of Orthodoxy. At this point, we would like to say that in the face of great changes taking place in lands that have an Orthodox presence, and before so many kinds of unstable conditions on a worldwide scale, the One, Holy, Catholic, and Apostolic, in other words Orthodox, Church should have strengthened the cohesion of the local Churches and given Herself over to the care of Her terror-stricken members and to their spiritual stabilization, on the one hand, and in Her consciousness [as the One Holy Church], on the other, She should have sounded the trumpet of Her unique redemptive power and Grace and manifested it before fallen humanity.

In this spirit, to the extent that our monastic office permits us, we closely follow developments in the so-called ecumenical movement and dialogues. We note that at times the word of Truth is rightly divided and, at times, compromises and concessions are made regarding fundamental matters of the Faith.

---

[3]In the Greek text that appeared in *Orthodox Typos* there is an apparent typographical error and this word was simply "united," although the context of the complete sentence clearly implies the word "disunited."

I. Thus, actions and declarations which representatives of Orthodox Churches have engaged in, that were unheard of until today and are altogether contrary to our holy Faith, have caused us deep sorrow.

We shall cite first the case of His Beatitude [Parthenios], the Patriarch of Alexandria, who, on at least two occasions, has stated that we Christians ought to recognize Mohammed as a prophet. To this day, however, no one has called for him to step down, and this dreadfully heedless Patriarch continues to preside in the Church of Alexandria as if there were nothing wrong.[4]

Second, we cite the case of the Patriarchate of Antioch, which, without a Pan-Orthodox decision, has proceeded to ecclesiastical communion with the Non-Chalcedonians [Monophysites].[5] This was done despite the fact that a most serious issue has not yet been resolved. It is the latter's non-acceptance of the Ecumenical Councils after the Third and, in particular, the Fourth, the Council of Chalcedon, which in fact constitutes an immovable basis of Orthodoxy. Unfortunately, in this case, too, we have not seen a single protest by other Orthodox Churches.

---

[4]Patriarch Parthenios has since passed away. Keep in mind, that the Christians of Egypt face terrible persecutions at the hands of the Moslem majority. This does not excuse the patriarch's absurd — even blasphemous — statement, but it does at least provide some context.

[5]This is a very thorny issue. While it appears that the Church of Antioch has authorized some intercommunion with the Syrian (Jacobite) Church on a limited basis, a union of Churches and full communion has *not* been effected.

The gravest matter, however, is the unacceptable change in the position of the Orthodox that arises from the joint statement at the June 1993 Balamand Conference of the mixed commission for the dialogue between Roman Catholics and Orthodox. It adopted anti-Orthodox positions, and it is mainly to this that we call the attention of Your All Holiness.

First, we must confess that the statements which Your All Holiness has made from time to time that the Uniate movement is an insurmountable obstacle to the continuation of the dialogue between Orthodox and Roman Catholics until now put us at ease.

But the above document [of Balamand] gives the impression that your statements are being sidestepped. Furthermore, Unia is receiving amnesty and is invited to the table of theological dialogue despite the contrary decision of the Third Pan-Orthodox Conference in Rhodes requiring:

> ... the complete withdrawal from Orthodox lands by the Uniate agents and propagandists of the Vatican; the incorporation of the so-called Uniate Churches and their subjection under the Church of Rome before the inauguration of the dialogue, because Unia and dialogue at the same time are irreconcilable.

II. Your All Holiness, the greatest scandal, however, is caused by the ecclesiological positions in the document. We shall refer here to fundamental deviations only.

In Paragraph 10 we read:

The Catholic Church... (which conducted missionary work against the Orthodox and) presented herself as the only one to whom salvation was entrusted. As a reaction, the Orthodox Church, in turn, came to accept the same vision according to which only in her could salvation be found. To assure the salvation of "the separated brethren" it even happened that Christians were rebaptized and that certain requirements of the religious freedom of persons and of their act of faith were forgotten. This perspective was one to which that period showed little sensitivity.

As Orthodox, we cannot accept this view. It was not as a reaction against Unia that our Holy Orthodox Church began to believe that She exclusively possessed salvation, but She believed it before Unia existed, from the time of the Schism, which took place for reasons of dogma. The Orthodox Church did not await the coming of Unia in order to acquire the consciousness that She is the unadulterated continuation of the One, Holy, Catholic, and Apostolic Church of Christ, because She has always had this self-awareness just as She had the awareness that the Papacy was in heresy.

If She did not use the term heresy frequently, it was because, according to Saint Mark of Ephesus, "The Latins are not only schismatics but heretics as well. However, the Church was silent on this because their race is large and more powerful than ours... and we wished not to fall into triumphalism over the Latins as heretics but to be accepting of their return and to cultivate brotherliness."

But when the Uniates and the agents of Rome were let loose on us in the East in order to proselytize the suffering Orthodox by mainly unlawful means, as they do even today, Orthodoxy was obliged to declare that truth, not for purposes of proselytism but in order to protect the flock.

Saint Photios repeatedly characterizes the Filioque as a heresy, and its believers as *cacodox* [wrongly believing].

Saint Gregory Palamas says of the Westerner Barlaam, that when he came to Orthodoxy, "He did not accept sanctifying water from our Church... to wipe away [his] stains from the West." Saint Gregory obviously considers him a heretic in need of sanctifying grace in order to come into the Orthodox Church.

The statement in the paragraph in question unjustly heaps responsibility on the Orthodox Church in order to lessen the responsibilities of the Papists. When did the Orthodox trample upon the religious freedom of the Uniates and Roman Catholics by baptizing them against their will? And if there were some exceptions, the Orthodox who signed the Balamand document forget that those who were rebaptized against their wishes were descendants of the Orthodox who were forcibly made Uniates, as occurred in Poland, Ukraine, and Moldavia (See Paragraph 11).

In Paragraph 13 we read:

> In fact, especially since the Pan-Orthodox Conferences began and since the Second Vatican Council, the rediscovery and the giving of proper value to the Church as communion, both on the part of Or-

thodox and of Catholics, has radically altered perspectives and thus attitudes. On each side it is recognized that what Christ has entrusted to his Church—profession of apostolic faith, participation in the same sacraments, above all the one priesthood celebrating the one sacrifice of Christ, the apostolic succession of bishops—cannot be the exclusive property of one of our Churches. In this context, it is clear that every form of rebaptism must be avoided.

The new discovery of the Church as communion by Roman Catholics has, of course, some significance for them who had no way out of the dilemma of their totalitarian ecclesiology and, therefore, had to turn their system of thought to the communal character of the Church. Thus, alongside the one extreme of totalitarianism, they place the other of collegiality, always motivated on the same man-centered level. The Orthodox Church, however, has always had the consciousness that She is not a simple communion but a theanthropic communion or a "communion of *theosis* [deification]," as Saint Gregory Palamas says in his homily on the procession of the Holy Spirit. Moreover, the communion of theosis is not only unknown in but also irreconcilable with Roman Catholic theology, which rejects [the doctrine of] the uncreated energies of God that form and sustain this communion.

Given these truths, it was with deepest sadness that we confirmed that this paragraph [13] makes the Orthodox Church equal to the Roman Catholic Church which abides in *cacodoxy* [wrong belief].

APPENDIX A

Serious theological differences, such as the *Filioque*, Papal primacy and infallibility, created grace, etc., are receiving amnesty, and a union is being forged without agreement in dogma.

Thus are verified the premonitions that the union designed by the Vatican, in which, as Saint Mark of Ephesus said, "the willing are unwittingly being manipulated," (i.e., the Orthodox, who also live under hostile circumstances ethnically and politically today and are captive to nations of other religions), is pushed to take place without agreement regarding doctrinal differences. The plan is for union to take place, despite the differences, through the mutual recognition of the Mysteries and apostolic succession of each Church, and the application of intercommunion, limited at first and broader later. After this, doctrinal differences can be discussed only as theological *opinions*.

But once union takes place, what sense is there in discussing theological differences? Rome knows that the Orthodox will never accept her alien teachings. Experience has proven this in the various attempts at union up to the present. Therefore, despite the differences, Rome is crafting a union and hoping, from a humanistic point of view (as her perspective always is), that, as the more powerful factor, in time she will absorb the weaker one, that is, Orthodoxy. Father John Romanides presaged this in his article "The Uniate Movement and Popular Ecumenism," in *The Orthodox Witness*, February 1966.

We would like to put these questions to the Orthodox who signed this document:

Do the *Filioque*, [Papal] primacy and infallibility, purgatory, the Immaculate Conception, and created grace constitute an apostolic confession? Despite all of this, is it possible for us Orthodox to recognize as apostolic the faith and confession of the Roman Catholics?

Do these serious theological deviations of Rome amount to heresies or not?

If they are, as they have been described by Orthodox Councils and fathers, do they not result in the invalidity of the Mysteries and the apostolic succession of heterodox and cacodox of this kind?

Is it possible for the fullness of Grace to exist where there is not the fullness of truth?

Is it possible to distinguish Christ of the truth from Christ of the Mysteries and apostolic succession?

Apostolic succession was first set forth by the Church as a historic confirmation of the continuous preservation of her truth. But when the truth itself is distorted, what meaning can a formulistic preservation of apostolic succession have? Did not the great heresiarchs often have this kind of external succession? How can it be possible for them to also be regarded as bearers of Grace?

And how is it possible for two Churches to be considered "Sister Churches" not because of their pre-Schism common descent but because of their so-called common confession, sanctifying Grace, and priesthood despite their great differences in dogmas?

Who among the Orthodox can accept as the true successor to the Apostles the infallible one, the one with the primacy of authority to rule over the entire Church and to be the religious and secular leader of the Vatican State?

Would this not be a denial of Apostolic Faith and Tradition?

Or are the signers of this document unaware that many Roman Catholics today groan under the foot of the Pope (and his scholastic, man-centered ecclesiological system) and desire to come into Orthodoxy?

How can these people who are tormented spiritually and desire holy Baptism not be received into Orthodoxy because the same Grace is supposedly both here and there? Ought we not, at that point, to respect their religious freedom, as the Balamand declaration demands in another circumstance, and grant them Orthodox Baptism? What defense shall we present to the Lord if we withhold the fullness of Grace from them who, after years of agony and personal searching, desire the holy Baptism of our One, Holy, Catholic, and Apostolic Church?

Paragraph 14 of the document quotes Pope John Paul II: "The ecumenical endeavor of the Sister Churches of East and West, grounded in dialogue and prayer, is the search for perfect and total communion which is neither absorption nor fusion but a meeting in truth and love."

But how is a union in the truth possible when differences in dogmas are sidestepped and both Churches are described as sisters despite the differences?

The Truth of the Church is indivisible because it is Christ Himself. But when there are differences in dogmas there cannot be unity in Christ.

From what we know about Church History, Churches were called Sister Churches when they held the same faith. Never was the Orthodox Church called a sister of any heterodox churches, regardless of the degree of heterodoxy or *cacodoxy* they held.

We ask ourselves a basic question: have religious syncretism and doctrinal minimalism—the byproducts of secularization and humanism—perhaps influenced the Orthodox signers of the document?

It is apparent that the document adopts, perhaps for the first time by the Orthodox side, the position that two Churches, the Orthodox and Roman Catholic, together constitute the One Holy Church or are two legitimate expressions of her.

Unfortunately, it is the first time that Orthodox have officially accepted a form of the branch theory.

Permit us to express our deep sorrow over this in as much as this theory comes into screaming conflict with Orthodox Tradition and Consciousness until now.

We have many witnesses to the Orthodox Consciousness that our Church alone constitutes the One Holy Church, and they are recognized as pan-Orthodox in authority. They are the:

1. Council of Constantinople, 1722;

2. Council of Constantinople, 1727;

3. Council of Constantinople, 1838;

4. 1848 Encyclical of the Four Patriarchs of the East and their synods;[6]

5. Council of Constantinople, 1895.

These decreed that only our Holy Orthodox Church constitutes the One Holy Church.

The 1895 Council of Constantinople summarizes all of the preceding Councils:

> Orthodoxy, that is, the Eastern Church, justly boasts in Christ that she is the Church of the Seven Ecumenical Councils and the first nine centuries of Christianity and is therefore the One, Holy, Catholic, and Apostolic Church of Christ, the 'pillar and bulwark of truth.' And the present Roman Church is the church of innovationism and adulteration of the writings of the Church Fathers and the distortion of the Holy Scriptures and the decrees of the Holy Councils. Justly and for good reason it was denounced and is denounced as long as it persists in its delusion. 'Better a praiseworthy war,' says Saint Gregory of Nazianzus, 'than a peace separated from God.'

Representatives of the Orthodox Churches declared the same things at World Council of Churches conferences. Among them were distinguished Orthodox theologians, such as Father Georges Florovsky. Thus, at the Conference of Lund in 1952, it was declared:

> We came here not to judge other Churches but to help them see the truth, to enlighten their thought in a brotherly manner, informing them of the

6The text of this Encyclical appears below in Appendix D.

teachings of the One, Holy, Catholic and Apostolic Church, that is to say, the Greek Orthodox Church, which is unaltered from the apostolic period.

At Evanston in 1954:

In conclusion, we are obliged to declare our deep conviction that the Holy Orthodox Church alone has preserved 'the faith once delivered unto the saints' in all of its fullness and purity. And this is not because of any human merit of ours but because God is pleased to preserve His treasure in earthen vessels. . .

And at New Delhi in 1961:

Unity has been broken and it is necessary that it be won anew. For the Orthodox Church is not a Confession, not one of the many or one among the many. For the Orthodox, the Orthodox Church is the Church. The Orthodox Church has the perception and consciousness that her inner structure and teaching coincide with the apostolic kerygma and the tradition of the ancient, undivided Church. The Orthodox Church exists in the unbroken and continuous succession of the sacramental ministry, of the sacramental life, and of the faith. The apostolic succession of the episcopal office and the sacramental ministry, for the Orthodox, is truly a component of the essence and, for this reason, a necessary element in the existence of the whole Church. In accordance with her inner conviction and an awareness of the circumstances, the Orthodox Church occupies a special and extraordinary position in divided Christendom as the bearer and witness of the tradition of the ancient, undivided

Church, from which the present Christian denominations originate by way of reduction and separation.

We could also set forth here the testimonies of the most distinguished and widely acknowledged Orthodox theologians. We shall limit ourselves to one, the late Father Demetrios Staniloae, a theologian distinguished not only for his wisdom but for the breadth and Orthodox mindset of [his] ecumenical perspective.

In many places of his noteworthy book, *Towards an Orthodox Ecumenism*, he refers to themes that are relevant to the joint statement [being discussed here] and bears Orthodox witness. Through it, therefore, the disagreement between the positions taken in the document and the Orthodox faith shall be shown:

> Without unity of faith and without communion in the same Body and Blood of the Incarnate Word, such a Church could not exist, nor could [it be] a Church in the full meaning of the word.

> In the case of one who is entering into full communion of faith with the members of the Orthodox Church and is becoming a member, *economia* [dispensation] is understood to give validity to a Mystery previously performed outside of the Church.

> In the Roman Catholic view, the Church is not so much a spiritual organism that is headed by Christ as it is a nomocanonical organization which, even

in the best of circumstances, lives not in the divine but in the supernatural[7] level of created grace.

In the preservation of this unity, an indispensable role is played by the unity of faith because the latter wholly bonds the members with Christ and with one another.

Those who confess not a whole and integral Christ but only certain parts of Him cannot achieve a complete communion either with the Church or with one another.

How it is possible for the Catholics to unite with the Orthodox in a common Eucharist when they believe that unity is derived more from the Pope than from the Holy Eucharist? Can love for the world spring forth from the Pope, that is, the love which springs from the Christ of the Holy Eucharist?

There is a growing recognition of the fact that Orthodoxy, as the complete body of Christ, reaches out in a concrete way to take in the parts that were separated.

It is self-evident that two complete bodies of Christ cannot exist.

III. Your All Holiness, one has to wonder why the Orthodox proceed to make these concessions while the

---

[7]In the Western context here, the supernatural which man experiences or participates in, like created grace, refers to something that is not uncreated: "What is received in the creature must itself be created." *Catholic Encyclopedia*, Vol. 13, New York, 1967, p. 815.

Roman Catholics not only persist in but reinforce their pope-centered ecclesiology.

It is a fact that the Second Vatican Council [1963] not only neglected to minimize the primacy and infallibility [of the Pope], indeed, it magnified these. According to the late Professor John Karmiris,

> Despite the fact that the Second Vatican Council covered over the familiar Latin claims about the Papacy's monarchical absolute rule with the mantle of the collegiality of the bishops, not only were those claims not diminished; on the contrary, they were reinforced by this Council. The present Pope [John XXIII] does not hesitate to promote them, even at inopportune times, with much emphasis.

And the Pope's Encyclical, "To the Bishops of the Catholic Church" (May 28, 1992), recognizes only Rome as the "catholic" church and the Pope as the only "catholic" bishop. The church of Rome and her bishop compose the "essence" of all other churches. Moreover, every local church and her bishop simply constitute expressions of the direct "presence" and "authority" of the bishop of Rome and his church, which determines from within every local church's ecclesial identity.

According to this papal document, since the Orthodox Churches refuse to submit to the Pope, they do not bear the character of the Church at all and are simply viewed as "partial churches." "*Verdienen der titel teilkirchen.*"

The same ecclesiology is expressed in *The Ecumenical Guide* ("a guide for the application of principles and agenda regarding ecumenism") of the Roman Catholic

Church, presented by Cardinal Cassidy to the meeting of Roman Catholic bishops (May 10-15, 1993, one month before Balamand), with non-Catholics and indeed Orthodox in attendance.

The Ecumenical Guide stresses that Roman Catholics "maintain the firm conviction that the singular Church of Christ subsists in the Catholic Church, which is ruled by the successor to Peter and by bishops who are in communion with him," inasmuch as the "College of Bishops has as its head the Bishop of Rome, the successor to Peter."

In the same document, many nice-sounding things are said about the need to develop an ecumenical dialogue and ecumenical education—obviously to muddy the waters and draw away naïve Orthodox by that effective, Vatican-designed method of unity, i.e., of submission to Rome.

The method, according to The Ecumenical Guide, is the following:

> The criteria that were established for ecumenical collaboration, on the one hand, are mutual recognition of baptism and the placement of the common symbols of faith in empirical liturgical life; and on the other, are collaboration in ecumenical education, joint prayer, and pastoral cooperation in order that we may be moved from conflict to coexistence, from coexistence to collaboration, from collaboration to sharing, from sharing to communion.

Such documents, however, that are full of hypocrisy are generally received as positive by the Orthodox.

We are saddened to ascertain that the joint declaration is founded upon the above Roman Catholic reasoning. Because of these recent developments under such terms, however, we begin to ask ourselves if those who claim that the various dialogues are detrimental to Orthodoxy might be justified after all.

Most Holy Father and *Despota*, in human terms, by means of that joint declaration Roman Catholics have succeeded in gaining from certain Orthodox recognition as the legitimate continuation of the One Holy Church with the fullness of Truth, Grace, Priesthood, Mysteries, and Apostolic Succession.

But that success is to their own detriment because it removes from them the possibility of acknowledging and repenting of their grave ecclesiology and doctrinal illness. For this reason, the concessions by Orthodox are not philanthropic. They are not for the good of either the Roman Catholics or the Orthodox. They jump from the hope of the Gospel (Col. 1:23) of Christ, the only God-Man, to the Pope, the man-god and idol of Western humanism.

For the sake of the Roman Catholics and the whole world, whose only hope is unadulterated Orthodoxy, we are obliged never to accept union or the description of the Roman Catholic Church as a "Sister Church," or the Pope as the canonical bishop of Rome, or the "Church" of Rome as having canonical Apostolic Succession, Priesthood, and Mysteries without their [the Papists'] expressly stated renunciation of the *Filioque*, the infallibility and primacy of the Pope, created grace, and the rest of their *cacodoxies*. For we shall never regard these as unimportant differences or mere theological opinions, but as differences that irrevocably debase the theanthropic character of the Church and introduce blasphemies.

The following decisions of Vatican II are typical:

The Roman Pontiff, the successor to Peter, is the permanent and visible source and foundation of the unity of the bishops and of the multitude of the faithful.

This religious submission of the will and mind must be manifested in a special way before the authentic teaching authority of the Roman Pontiff, even when he is not speaking *ex cathedra*.

The Roman Pontiff, the head of the college of bishops, by virtue of his office, possesses infallibility when, strengthening his brethren (Luke 23:32) as the shepherd and highest teacher of all the faithful, he declares a teaching through an act of definition regarding faith or morals. For this reason it is justly said that the decrees of the Pope are irreversible in nature and not subject to dispensation by the Church inasmuch as they were pronounced with the collaboration of the Holy Spirit... Consequently, the decrees of the Pope are subject to no other approval, to no other appeal, to no other judgment. For the Roman Pontiff does not express his opinion as a private person but as the highest teacher of the universal Church, upon whom personally rests the gift of the infallibility of the very Church herself and who sets forth and protects the teaching of the Catholic Faith.

In the course of his responsibility as the vicar of Christ and shepherd of the whole Church, the Roman Pontiff has the fullest, highest, and universal authority in the Church, which he is always empowered to exercise freely... There cannot exist an Ecumenical Council if it is not validated or at least accepted by the successor to Peter. The convocation, presidency, and approval of the decisions of the Councils are the prerogative of the Roman Pontiff.

Do all of these teachings, Your All Holiness, not fall upon Orthodox ears as blasphemy against the Holy Spirit and against the Divine Builder of the Church, Jesus Christ, the only eternal and infallible Head of the Church from Whom alone springs forth the unity of the Church? Do these not utterly contradict the Gospel-centered and God-Man-centered Orthodox Ecclesiology inspired by the Holy Spirit? Do they not subordinate the God-Man to man?

How can we make concessions or co-exist with such a spirit without losing our faith and salvation?

Remaining faithful to all that we have received from our Holy Fathers, we shall never accept the present Roman "Church" as co-representative with ours of the One, Holy, Catholic, and Apostolic Church of Christ.

We consider it necessary that among the theological differences the distinction between the essence and the energy of God, and the uncreatedness of the divine energies be noted, because if Grace is created, as the Roman Catholics claim, salvation and the *theosis* of man is nullified, and the Church ceases to be a communion of *theosis* and degenerates into a nomocanonical institution.

Deeply pained in our soul because of all the above, we have recourse to you our Spiritual Father. And with deepest respect, we call upon you and implore you, in your characteristic pastoral understanding and sensitivity, to take this most grave matter in hand and not accept the [Balamand] document, and generally to take every possible action to stave off the undesirable consequences it will have for pan-Orthodox unity if by chance some Churches adopt it.

Moreover, we ask for your holy and God-obedient prayers so that we too who are lowly inhabitants and monastics of the Holy Mountain, in this time of spiritual confusion, compromise, secularization, and the dulling of our doctrinal acuity, may remain faithful unto death to that which was passed on to us by our Holy Fathers as a form of doctrine (Rom. 6:17), whatever that may cost us.

With deepest respect, we venerate your holy right hand.

Signed by: All Representatives and Presidents of the twenty Sacred Monasteries of the Holy Mountain of Athos

PS. Note that this letter was also sent to the Churches that participated in the theological dialogue and are, therefore, directly concerned, and to the remaining Churches to keep them informed.

Encyclical of the Eastern Patriarchs, 1848

A Reply by the patriarchs of Constantinople, Alexandria, Antioch, and Jerusalem to the Epistle of Pope Pius IX, "to the Easterns."

To All the Bishops Everywhere, Beloved in the Holy Spirit, Our Venerable, Most Dear Brethren; and to their Most Pious Clergy; and to All the Genuine Orthodox Sons of the One, Holy, Catholic and Apostolic Church:

Brotherly Salutation in the Holy Spirit, and Every Good from God, and Salvation.

1. The holy, evangelical and divine Gospel of Salvation should be set forth by all in its original simplicity, and should evermore be believed in its unadulterated purity, even the same as it was revealed to His holy Apostles by our Savior, who for this very cause, descending from the bosom of God the Father, *made Himself of no reputation and took upon Him the form of a servant* (Phil. ii. 7); even the same, also, as those Apostles, who were ear and eye witnesses, sounded it forth, like clear-toned trumpets, to all that are under the sun (*for their sound is gone out into all lands, and their words into the ends of the world*); and, last of all, the very same as the many great and glorious Fathers of the Catholic Church

in all parts of the earth, who heard those Apostolic voices, both by their synodical and their individual teachings handed it down to all everywhere, and even unto us. But the Prince of Evil, that spiritual enemy of man's salvation, as formerly in Eden, craftily assuming the pretext of profitable counsel, he made man to become a transgressor of the divinely-spoken command. So in the spiritual Eden, the Church of God, he has from time to time beguiled many; and, mixing the deleterious drugs of heresy with the clear streams of orthodox doctrine, gives of the potion to drink to many of the innocent who live unguardedly, not giving earnest heed to the things they have heard (Heb. ii. 10), and to what they have been told by their fathers (Deut. xxxii. 7), in accordance with the Gospel and in agreement with the ancient Doctors; and who, imagining that the preached and written Word of the LORD and the perpetual witness of His Church are not sufficient for their souls' salvation, impiously seek out novelties, as we change the fashion of our garments, embracing a counterfeit of the evangelical doctrine.

2. Hence have arisen manifold and monstrous heresies, which the Catholic Church, even from her infancy, taking unto her *the whole armor of God*, and assuming *the sword of the Spirit, which is the Word of God* (Eph. vi. 13-17,) has been compelled to combat. She has triumphed over all unto this day, and she will triumph forever, being manifested as mightier and more illustrious after each struggle.

3. Of these heresies, some already have entirely failed, some are in decay, some have wasted away,

some yet flourish in a greater or less degree vigorous until the time of their return to the Faith, while others are reproduced to run their course from their birth to their destruction. For being the miserable cogitations and devices of miserable men, both one and the other, struck with the thunderbolt of the anathema of the seven Ecumenical Councils, shall vanish away, though they may last a thousand years; for the orthodoxy of the Catholic and Apostolic Church, by the living Word of God, alone endures for ever, according to the infallible promise of the LORD: *the gates of hell shall not prevail against it* (Matt. xviii. 18). Certainly, the mouths of ungodly and heretical men, however bold, however plausible and fair-speaking, however smooth they may be, will not prevail against the orthodox doctrine winning its way silently and without noise. But, *wherefore doth the way of the wicked prosper?* (Jer. xii. 1.) *Why are the ungodly exalted and lifted up as the cedars of Lebanon* (Ps. xxxvii. 35), to defile the peaceful worship of God? The reason of this is mysterious, and the Church, though daily praying that this cross, this messenger of Satan, may depart from her, ever hears from the Lord: *My grace is sufficient for thee, my strength is made perfect in weakness* (2. Cor. xii. 9). Wherefore she gladly glories in her infirmities, that the power of Christ may rest upon her, and that they which are approved may be made manifest (1. Cor. x. 19).

4. Of these heresies diffused, with what sufferings the LORD hath known, over a great part of the world, was formerly Arianism, and at present is the Papacy. This, too, as the former has become extinct, although

now flourishing, shall not endure, but pass away and be cast down, *and a great voice from heaven shall cry: It is cast down* (Rev. xii. 10).

5. The new doctrine, that "the Holy Spirit proceedeth from the Father and the Son," is contrary to the memorable declaration of our LORD, emphatically made respecting it: *which proceedeth from the Father* (John xv. 26), and contrary to the universal Confession of the Catholic Church as witnessed by the seven Ecumenical Councils, uttering "which proceedeth from the Father." (Symbol of Faith).

> i. This novel opinion destroys the oneness from the One cause, and the diverse origin of the Persons of the Blessed Trinity, both of which are witnessed to in the Gospel.

> ii. Even into the divine *Hypostases* or Persons of the Trinity, of equal power and equally to be adored, it introduces diverse and unequal relations, with a confusion or commingling of them.

> iii. It reproaches as imperfect, dark, and difficult to be understood, the previous Confession of the One Holy Catholic and Apostolic Church.

> iv. It censures the holy Fathers of the first Ecumenical Synod of Nice and of the second Ecumenical Synod at Constantinople, as imperfectly expressing what relates to the Son and Holy Sprit, as if they had been silent respecting the peculiar property of each Person of the Godhead, when it was necessary that all their divine properties should be expressed against the Arians and Macedonians.

v. It reproaches the Fathers of the third, fourth, fifth, sixth, and seventh Ecumenical Councils, which had published over the world a divine Creed, perfect and complete, and interdicted under dread anathemas and penalties not removed, all addition, or diminution, or alteration, or variation in the smallest particular of it, by themselves or any whomsoever. Yet was this quickly to be corrected and augmented, and consequently the whole theological doctrine of the Catholic Fathers was to be subjected to change, as if, forsooth, a new property even in regard to the three Persons of the Blessed Trinity had been revealed.

vi. It clandestinely found an entrance at first in the Churches of the West, "a wolf in sheep's clothing," that is, under the signification not of procession, according to the Greek meaning in the Gospel and the Creed, but under the signification of mission, as Pope Martin explained it to the Confessor Maximus, and as Anastasius the Librarian explained it to John VIII.

vii. It exhibits incomparable boldness, acting without authority, and forcibly puts a false stamp upon the Creed, which is the common inheritance of Christianity.

viii. It has introduced huge disturbances into the peaceful Church of God, and divided the nations.

ix. It was publicly proscribed, at its first promulgation, by two ever-to-be-remembered Popes, Leo III and John VIII, the latter of whom, in his epistle to the blessed Photius, classes with Judas those who first brought the interpolation into the Creed.

x. It has been condemned by many Holy Councils of the four Patriarchs of the East.

xi. It was subjected to anathema, as a novelty and augmentation of the Creed, by the eighth Ecumenical Council, congregated at Constantinople for the pacification of the Eastern and Western Churches.

xii. As soon as it was introduced into the Churches of the West it brought forth disgraceful fruits, bringing with it, little by little, other novelties, for the most part contrary to the express commands of our Savior in the Gospel—commands which till its entrance into the Churches were closely observed. Among these novelties may be numbered sprinkling instead of baptism, denial of the divine Cup to the Laity, elevation of one and the same bread broken, the use of wafers, unleavened instead of real bread, the disuse of the Benediction in the Liturgies, even of the sacred Invocation of the All-holy and Consecrating Spirit, the abandonment of the old Apostolic Mysteries of the Church, such as not anointing baptized infants, or their not receiving the Eucharist, the exclusion of married men from the Priesthood, the infallibility of the Pope and his claim as Vicar of Christ, and the like. Thus it was that the interpolation led to the setting aside of the old Apostolic pattern of well nigh all the Mysteries and all doctrine, a pattern which the ancient, holy, and orthodox Church of Rome kept, when she was the most honored part of the Holy, Catholic and Apostolic Church.

xiii. It drove the theologians of the West, as its defenders, since they had no ground either in Scripture or the Fathers to countenance heretical teachings, not only into misrepresentations of the Scriptures, such as are seen in none of the Fathers of the Holy Catholic Church, but also into adulterations of the sacred and pure writings of the Fathers alike of the East and West.

xiv. It seemed strange, unheard of, and blasphemous, even to those reputed Christian communions, which, before its origin, had been for other just causes for ages cut off from the Catholic fold.

xv. It has not yet been even plausibly defended out of the Scriptures, or with the least reason out of the Fathers, from the accusations brought against it, notwithstanding all the zeal and efforts of its supporters. The doctrine bears all the marks of error arising out of its nature and peculiarities. All erroneous doctrine touching the Catholic truth of the Blessed Trinity, and the origin of the divine Persons, and the subsistence of the Holy Spirit, is and is called heresy, and they who so hold are deemed heretics, according to the sentence of St. Damasus, Pope of Rome, who says: "If any one rightly holds concerning the Father and the Son, yet holds not rightly of the Holy Spirit, he is an heretic" (Cath. Conf. of Faith which Pope Damasus sent to Paulinus, Bishop of Thessalonica). Wherefore the One, Holy, Catholic, and Apostolic Church, following in the steps of the holy Fathers, both Eastern and Western, proclaimed of old to our progenitors and again teaches today synodically, that the said novel doctrine of the Holy Spirit proceeding from the Father and the Son is essentially heresy, and its maintainers, whoever they be, are heretics, according to the sentence of Pope St. Damasus, and that the congregations of such are also heretical, and that all spiritual communion in worship of the orthodox sons of the Catholic Church with such is unlawful. Such is the force of the seventh Canon of the third Ecumenical Council.

6. This heresy, which has united to itself many innovations, as has been said, appeared about the middle of the seventh century, at first and secretly, and then under various disguises, over the Western Provinces of Europe, until by degrees, creeping along for four or five centuries, it obtained precedence over the ancient orthodoxy of those parts, through the heedlessness of Pastors and the countenance of Princes. Little by little it overspread not only the hitherto orthodox Churches of Spain, but also the German, and French, and Italian Churches, whose orthodoxy at one time was sounded throughout the world, with whom our divine Fathers such as the great Athanasius and heavenly Basil conferred, and whose sympathy and fellowship with us until the seventh Ecumenical Council, preserved unharmed the doctrine of the Catholic and Apostolic Church. But in process of time, by envy of the devil, the novelties respecting the sound and orthodox doctrine of the Holy Spirit, the blasphemy of whom shall not be forgiven unto men either in this world or the next, ac-

cording to the saying of our Lord (Matt. xii. 32), and others that succeeded respecting the divine Mysteries, particularly that of the world-saving Baptism, and the Holy Communion, and the Priesthood, like prodigious births, overspread even Old Rome; and thus sprung, by assumption of special distinctions in the Church as a badge and title, the Papacy. Some of the Bishops of that City, styled Popes, for example Leo III and John VIII, did indeed, as has been said, denounce the innovation, and published the denunciation to the world, the former by those silver plates, the latter by his letter to the holy Photius at the eighth Ecumenical Council, and another to Sphendopulcrus, by the hands of Methodius, Bishop of Moravia. The greater part, however, of their successors, the Popes of Rome, enticed by the antisynodical privileges offered them for the oppression of the Churches of God, and finding in them much worldly advantage, and "much gain," and conceiving a Monarchy in the Catholic Church and a monopoly of the gifts of the Holy Spirit, changed the ancient worship at will, separating themselves by novelties from the old received Christian Polity. Nor did they cease their endeavors, by lawless projects (as veritable history assures us), to entice the other four Patriarchates into their apostasy from Orthodoxy, and so subject the Catholic Church to the whims and ordinances of men.

7. Our illustrious predecessors and fathers, with united labor and counsel, seeing the evangelical doctrine received from the Fathers to be trodden under foot, and the robe of our Savior woven from above to be torn by wicked hands, and stimulated by fatherly and

brotherly love, wept for the desolation of so many Christians for whom Christ died. They exercised much zeal and ardor, both synodically and individually, in order that the orthodox doctrine of the Holy Catholic Church being saved, they might knit together as far as they were able that which had been rent; and like approved physicians they consulted together for the safety of the suffering member, enduring many tribulations, and contempts, and persecutions, if haply the Body of Christ might not be divided, or the definitions of the divine and august Synods be made of none effect. But veracious history has transmitted to us the relentlessness of the Western perseverance in error. These illustrious men proved indeed on this point the truth of the words of our holy father Basil the sublime, when he said, from experience, concerning the Bishops of the West, and particularly of the Pope: "They neither know the truth nor endure to learn it, striving against those who tell them the truth, and strengthening themselves in their heresy" (to Eusebius of Samosata). Thus, after a first and second brotherly admonition, knowing their impenitence, shaking them off and avoiding them, they gave them over to their reprobate mind. "War is better than peace, apart from God," as said our Holy Father Gregory, concerning the Arians. From that time there has been no spiritual communion between us and them; for they have with their own hands dug deep the chasm between themselves and Orthodoxy.

Yet the Papacy has not on this account ceased to annoy the peaceful Church of God, but sending out everywhere so-called missionaries, men of reprobate

minds, it compasses land and sea to make one prose-
lyte, to deceive one of the Orthodox, to corrupt the doctrine of our LORD, to adulterate, by addition, the divine
Creed of our holy Faith, to prove the Baptism which
God gave us superfluous, the communion of the Cup
void of sacred efficacy, and a thousand other things
which the demon of novelty dictated to the all-daring
Schoolmen of the Middle Ages and to the Bishops of the
elder Rome, venturing all things through lust of power.
Our blessed predecessors and fathers, in their piety,
though tried and persecuted in many ways and means,
within and without, directly and indirectly, "yet confident in the LORD," were able to save and transmit to us
this inestimable inheritance of our fathers, which we
too, by the help of God, will transmit as a rich treasure
to the generations to come, even to the end of the
world. But notwithstanding this, the Papists do not
cease to this day, nor will cease, according to wont, to
attack Orthodoxy,—a daily living reproach which they
have before their eyes, being deserters from the faith of
their fathers. Would that they made these aggressions
against the heresy which has overspread and mastered
the West. For who doubts that had their zeal for the
overthrow of Orthodoxy been employed for the overthrow of heresy and novelties, agreeable to the God-
loving counsels of Leo III and John VIII, those glorious
and last Orthodox Popes, not a trace of it, long ago,
would have been remembered under the sun, and we
should now be saying the same things, according to the
Apostolic promise. But the zeal of those who succeeded
them was not for the protection of the Orthodox Faith,

in conformity with the zeal worthy of all remembrance which was in Leo III, now among the blessed.

9. In a measure the aggressions of the later Popes in their own persons had ceased, and were carried on only by means of missionaries. But lately, Pius IX, becoming Bishop of Rome and proclaimed Pope in 1847, published on the sixth of January, in this present year, an Encyclical Letter addressed to the Easterns, consisting of twelve pages in the Greek version, which his emissary has disseminated, like a plague coming from without, within our Orthodox Fold. In this Encyclical, he addresses those who at different times have gone over from different Christian Communions, and embraced the Papacy, and of course are favorable to him, extending his arguments also to the Orthodox, either particularly or without naming them; and, citing our divine and holy Fathers (p. 3, 1.14-18; p. 4, 1.19; p. 9, 1.6; and pp. 17, 23), he manifestly calumniates them and us their successors and descendants: them, as if they admitted readily the Papal commands and rescripts without question because issuing from the Popes as undoubted arbiters of the Catholic Church; us, as unfaithful to their examples (for thus he trespasses on the Fold committed to us by God), as severed from our Fathers, as careless of our sacred trusts, and of the soul's salvation of our spiritual children. Usurping as his own possession the Catholic Church of Christ, by occupancy, as he boasts, of the Episcopal Throne of St. Peter, he desires to deceive the more simple into apostasy from Orthodoxy, choosing for the basis of all theological instruction these paradoxical words (p. 10, 1.29): "nor is

there any reason why ye refuse a return to the true Church and Communion with this my holy Throne."

10. Each one of our brethren and sons in Christ who have been piously brought up and instructed, wisely regarding the wisdom given him from God, will decide that the words of the present Bishop of Rome, like those of his schismatical predecessors, are not words of peace, as he affirms (p. 7,1.8), and of benevolence, but words of deceit and guile, tending to self-aggrandizement, agreeably to the practice of his antisynodical predecessors. We are therefore sure, that even as heretofore, so hereafter the Orthodox will not be beguiled. *For the word of our LORD is sure* (John x. 5), A stranger will they not follow, but flee from him, for they know not the voice of strangers.

11. For all this we have esteemed it our paternal and brotherly need, and a sacred duty, by our present admonition to confirm you in the Orthodoxy you hold from your forefathers, and at the same time point out the emptiness of the syllogisms of the Bishop of Rome, of which he is manifestly himself aware. For not from his Apostolic Confession does he glorify his Throne, but from his Apostolic Throne seeks to establish his dignity, and from his dignity, his Confession. The truth is the other way. The Throne of Rome is esteemed that of St. Peter by a single tradition, but not from Holy Scripture, where the claim is in favor of Antioch, whose Church is therefore witnessed by the great Basil (Ep. 48 Athan.) to be "the most venerable of all the Churches in the world." Still more, the second Ecumenical Council, writing to a Council of the West (to the most honorable

and religious brethren and fellow-servants, Damasus, Ambrose, Britto, Valerian, and others), witnesseth, saying: "The oldest and truly Apostolic Church of Antioch, in Syria, where first the honored name of Christians was used." We say then that the Apostolic Church of Antioch had no right of exemption from being judged according to divine Scripture and synodical declarations, though truly venerated for the throne of St. Peter. But what do we say? The blessed Peter, even in his own person, was judged before all for the truth of the Gospel, and, as Scripture declares, was found blamable and not walking uprightly. What opinion is to be formed of those who glory and pride themselves solely in the possession of his Throne, so great in their eyes? Nay, the sublime Basil the great, the Ecumenical teacher of Orthodoxy in the Catholic Church, to whom the Bishops of Rome are obliged to refer us (p. 8, 1.31), has clearly and explicitly above (§ 7) shown us what estimation we ought to have of the judgments of the inaccessible Vatican: "They neither," he says, "know the truth, nor endure to learn it, striving against those who tell them the truth, and strengthening themselves in their heresy." So that these our holy Fathers whom his Holiness the Pope, worthily admiring as lights and teachers even of the West, accounts as belonging to us, and advises us (p. 8) to follow, teach us not to judge Orthodoxy from the holy Throne, but the Throne itself and him that is on the Throne by the sacred Scriptures, by Synodical decrees and limitations, and by the Faith which has been preached, even the Orthodoxy of continuous teaching. Thus did our Fathers judge and con-

demn Honorius, Pope of Rome, and Dioscorus, Pope of
Alexandria, and Macedonius and Nestorius, Patriarchs
of Constantinople, and Peter Gnapheus, Patriarch of
Antioch, with others. For if the abomination of desolation stood in the Holy Place, why not innovation and
heresy upon a holy Throne? Hence is exhibited in a
brief compass the weakness and feebleness of the efforts
in behalf of the despotism of the Pope of Rome. For,
unless the Church of Christ was founded upon the immovable rock of St. Peter's Confession, *Thou art the
Christ, the Son of the Living God* (which was the answer
of the Apostles in common, when the question was put
to them, *Whom say ye that I am?* (Matt. xvi. 15,) as the
Fathers, both Eastern and Western, interpret the passage to us), the Church was built upon a slippery foundation, even on Cephas himself, not to say on the Pope,
who, after monopolizing the Keys of the Kingdom of
Heaven, has made such an administration of them as is
plain from history. But our divine Fathers, with one accord, teach that the sense of the thrice-repeated command, Feed my sheep, implied no prerogative in St. Peter over the other Apostles, least of all in his successors.
It was a simple restoration to his Apostleship, from
which he had fallen by his thrice-repeated denial. St.
Peter himself appears to have understood the intention
of the thrice-repeated question of our Lord: *Lovest thou
Me more than these?* (John xxi. 15;) for, calling to mind
the words, *Though all shall be offended because of Thee, yet
will I never be offended* (Matt. xxvi. 33), he was grieved
because He said unto him the third time, *Lovest thou
Me?* But his successors, from self-interest, understand

the expression as indicative of St. Peter's more ready mind.

12. His Holiness the Pope says (p. viii. 1.12.) that our LORD said to Peter (Luke xxii. 32), *I have prayed for thee, that thy faith fail not: and when thou art converted, strengthen thy brethren.* Our LORD so prayed because Satan had sought to overthrow the faith of all the disciples, but the LORD allowed him Peter only, chiefly because he had uttered words of boasting, and justified himself above the rest (Matt. xxvi. 33): *Though all shall be offended, because of Thee, yet will I never be offended.* The permission to Satan was but temporary. He began to curse and to swear: *I know not the man.* So weak is human nature, left to itself. The spirit is willing, but the flesh is weak. It was but temporary, that, coming again to himself by his return in tears of repentance, he might the rather strengthen his brethren who had neither perjured themselves nor denied. Oh! The wise judgment of the LORD! How divine and mysterious was the last night of our Savior upon earth! That sacred Supper is believed to be consecrated to this day in every Church: *This do in remembrance of Me* (Luke xxii. 19), and *As often as ye eat this bread and drink this cup, ye do show the LORD's death till He come* (1 Cor. xi. 26). Of the brotherly love thus earnestly commended to us by the common Master, saying, *By this shall all men know that ye are My disciples, if ye have love one to another* (John xiii. 35), have the Popes first broken the stamp and seal, supporting and receiving heretical novelties, contrary to the things delivered to us and canonically confirmed by our Teachers and Fathers in common. This love acts

at this day with power in the souls of Christian people, and particularly in their leaders. We boldly avow before God and men, that the prayer of our Savior (p. ix. 1.43) to God and His Father for the common love and unity of Christians in the One Holy Catholic and Apostolic Church, in which we believe, *that they may be one, even as We are one* (John xvii. 22), worketh in us no less than in his Holiness. Our brotherly love and zeal meet that of his Holiness, with only this difference, that in us it worketh for the covenanted preservation of the pure, undefiled, divine, spotless, and perfect Creed of the Christian Faith, in conformity to the voice of the Gospel and the decrees of the seven holy Ecumenical Synods and the teachings of the ever-existing Catholic Church: but worketh in his Holiness to prop and strengthen the authority and dignity of them that sit on the Apostolic Throne, and their new doctrine. Behold then, the head and front, so to speak, of all the differences and disagreements that have happened between us and them, and the middle wall of partition, which we hope will be taken away in the time of his Holiness, and by the aid of his renowned wisdom, according to the promise of God (St. John x. 16): *Other sheep I have which are not of this fold: them also I must bring and they shall hear my voice* (*Who proceedeth from the Father*). Let it be said then, in the third place, that if it be supposed, according to the words of his Holiness, that this prayer of our LORD for Peter when about to deny and perjure himself, remained attached and united to the Throne of Peter, and is transmitted with power to those who from time to time sit upon it, although, as has before been said, nothing contributes to confirm the opinion (as we are strikingly assured from the example of the blessed Peter himself, even after the descent of the Holy Spirit) yet are we convinced from the words of our LORD, that the time will come when that divine prayer concerning the denial of Peter, "that his faith might not fail for ever" will operate also in some one of the successors of his Throne, who will also weep, as he did, bitterly, and being sometime converted will strengthen us, his brethren, still more in the Orthodox Confession, which we hold from our forefathers;—and would that his Holiness might be this true successor of the blessed Peter! To this our humble prayer, what hinders that we should add our sincere and hearty Counsel in the name of the Holy Catholic Church? We dare not say, as does his Holiness (p. x. 1.22), that it should be done "without any delay"; but without haste, after mature consideration, and also, if need be, after consultation with the more wise, religious, truth-loving, and prudent of the Bishops, Theologians, and Doctors, to be found at the present day, by God's good Providence, in every nation of the West.

13. His Holiness says that the Bishop of Lyons, St. Irenaeus, writes in praise of the Church of Rome: "That the whole Church, namely, the faithful from everywhere, must come together in that Church, because of its Primacy, in which Church the tradition, given by the Apostles, has in all respects been observed by the faithful everywhere." Although this saint says by no means what the followers of the Vatican would make out, yet even granting their interpretation, we reply: Who de-

231

nies that the ancient Roman Church was Apostolic and Orthodox? None of us will question that it was a model of orthodoxy. We will specially add, for its greater praise, from the historian Sozomen (Hist. Eccl. lib. iii. cap. 12), the passage, which his Holiness has over-looked, respecting the mode by which for a time she was enabled to preserve the orthodoxy which we praise: — "For, as everywhere," saith Sozomen, "the Church throughout the West, being guided purely by the doctrines of the Fathers, was delivered from conten-tion and deception concerning these things." Would any of the Fathers or ourselves deny her canonical privilege in the rank of the hierarchy, so long as she was guided purely by the doctrines of the Fathers, walking by the plain rule of Scripture and the holy Synods! But at present we do not find preserved in her the dogma of the Blessed Trinity according to the Creed of the holy Fathers assembled first in Nicea and after-wards in Constantinople, which the other five Ecu-menical Councils confessed and confirmed with such anathemas on those who adulterated it in the smallest particular, as if they had thereby destroyed it. Nor do we find the Apostolical pattern of holy Baptism, nor the Invocation of the consecrating Spirit upon the holy ele-ments: but we see in that Church the eucharistic Cup, heavenly drink, considered superfluous, (what profan-ity!) and very many other things, unknown not only to our holy Fathers, who were always entitled the catholic, clear rule and index of Orthodoxy, as his Holiness, re-vering the truth, himself teaches (p. vi), but also un-known to the ancient holy Fathers of the West. We see

that very primacy, for which his Holiness now contends
with all his might, as did his predecessors, transformed
from a brotherly character and hierarchical privilege
into a lordly superiority. What then is to be thought of
his unwritten traditions, if the written have undergone
such a change and alteration for the worse? Who is so
bold and confident in the dignity of the Apostolic
Throne, as to dare to say that if our holy Father, St. Irenaeus, were alive again, seeing it was fallen from the
ancient and primitive teaching in so many most essential and catholic articles of Christianity, he would not be
himself the first to oppose the novelties and self-
sufficient constitutions of that Church which was
lauded by him as guided purely by the doctrines of the
Fathers? For instance, when he saw the Roman Church
not only rejecting from her Liturgical Canon, according
to the suggestion of the Schoolmen, the very ancient
and Apostolic invocation of the Consecrating Spirit,
and miserably mutilating the Sacrifice in its most essential part, but also urgently hastening to cut it out from
the Liturgies of other Christian Communions also, — his
Holiness slanderously asserting, in a manner so unwor-
thy of the Apostolic Throne on which he boasts himself,
that it "crept in after the division between the East and
West" (p. xi. 1.11) — what would not the holy Father say
respecting this novelty? Irenaeus assures us (lib. iv. c.
34) "that bread, from the ground, receiving the evocation of God, is no longer common bread," etc., meaning
by "evocation" invocation: for that Irenaeus believed
the Mystery of the Sacrifice to be consecrated by means
of this invocation is especially remarked even by Fran-

ciscus Feu-Ardentius, of the order of popish monks
called Minorites, who in 1639 edited the writings of that
saint with comments, who says (lib. i. c. 18, p. 114,) that
Irenaeus teaches "that the bread and mixed cup become
the true Body and Blood of Christ by the words of invocation." Or, hearing of the vicarial and appellate jurisdiction of the Pope, what would not the Saint say, who,
for a small and almost indifferent question concerning
the celebration of Easter (Euseb. Eccl. Hist. v. 26), so
boldly and victoriously opposed and defeated the violence of Pope Victor in the free Church of Christ? Thus
he who is cited by his Holiness as a witness of the primacy of the Roman Church, shows that its dignity is
not that of a lordship, nor even appellate, to which St.
Peter himself was never ordained, but is a brotherly
privilege in the Catholic Church, and an honor assigned
the Popes on account of the greatness and privilege of
the City. Thus, also, the fourth Ecumenical Council, for
the preservation of the gradation in rank of Churches
canonically established by the third Ecumenical Council
(Canon 8), following the second (Canon 3), as that again
followed the first (Canon 6), which called the appellate
jurisdiction of the Pope over the West a Custom, thus
uttered its determination: "On account of that City being the Imperial City, the Fathers have with reason
given it prerogatives" (Canon 28). Here is nothing said
of the Pope's special monopoly of the Apostolicity of St.
Peter, still less of a vicarship in Rome's Bishops, and a
universal Pastorate. This deep silence in regard to such
great privileges—not only so, but the reason assigned
for the primacy, not *Feed my sheep*, not *On this rock will I*

build My Church, but simply old Custom, and the City being the Imperial City; and these things, not from the LORD, but from the Fathers—will seem, we are sure, a great paradox to his Holiness entertaining other ideas of his prerogatives. The paradox will be the greater, since, as we shall see, he greatly honors the said fourth Ecumenical Synod as one to be found a witness for his Throne; and St. Gregory, the eloquent, called the Great (lib. i. Ep. 25), was wont to speak of the four Ecumenical Councils [not the Roman See] as the four Gospels, and the four-sided stone on which the Catholic Church is built.

14. His Holiness says (p. ix. 1.12) that the Corinthians, divided among themselves, referred the matter to Clement, Pope of Rome, who wrote to them his decision on the case; and they so prized his decision that they read it in the Churches. But this event is a very weak support for the Papal authority in the house of God. For Rome being then the center of the Imperial Province and the chief City, in which the Emperors lived, it was proper that any question of importance, as history shows that of the Corinthians to have been, should be decided there, especially if one of the contending parties ran thither for external aid: as is done even to this day. The Patriarchs of Alexandria, Antioch, and Jerusalem, when unexpected points of difficulty arise, write to the Patriarch of Constantinople, because of its being the seat of Empire, as also on account of its synodical privileges; and if this brotherly aid shall rectify that which should be rectified, it is well; but if not, the matter is reported to the province, according to the estab-

lished system. But this brotherly agreement in Christian faith is not purchased by the servitude of the Churches of God. Let this be our answer also to the examples of a fraternal and proper championship of the privileges of Julius and Innocent Bishops of Rome, by St. Athanasius the Great and St. John Chrysostom, referred to by his Holiness (p. ix. 1. 6,17), for which their successors now seek to recompense us by adulterating the divine Creed. Yet was Julius himself indignant against some for "disturbing the Churches by not maintaining the doctrines of Nice" (Soz. Hist. Ec. lib. iii. c. 7), and threatening (id.) excommunication, "if they ceased not their innovations." In the case of the Corinthians, moreover, it is to be remarked that the Patriarchal Thrones being then but three, Rome was the nearer and more accessible to the Corinthians, to which, therefore, it was proper to have resort. In all this we see nothing extraordinary, nor any proof of the despotic power of the Pope in the free Church of God. §15. But, finally, his Holiness says (p. ix. 1.12) that the fourth Ecumenical Council (which by mistake he quite transfers from Chalcedon to Carthage), when it read the epistle of Pope Leo I, cried out, "Peter has thus spoken by Leo." It was so indeed. But his Holiness ought not to overlook how, and after what examination, our fathers cried out, as they did, in praise of Leo. Since however his Holiness, consulting brevity, appears to have omitted this most necessary point, and the manifest proof that an Ecumenical Council is not only above the Pope but above any Council of his, we will explain to the public the matter as it really happened. Of more than six hundred fathers assembled in the Council of Chalcedon, about two hundred of the wisest were appointed by the Council to examine both as to language and sense the said epistle of Leo; nor only so, but to give in writing and with their signatures their own judgment upon it, whether it were orthodox or not. These, about two hundred judgments and resolution on the epistle, as chiefly found in the Fourth Session of the said holy Council in such terms as the following: "Maximus of Antioch in Syria said, 'The epistle of the holy Leo, Archbishop of Imperial Rome, agrees with the decisions of the three hundred and eighteen holy fathers at Nicea, and the hundred and fifty at Constantinople, which is new Rome, and with the faith expounded at Ephesus by the most holy Bishop Cyril: and I have subscribed it.'"

And again: "Theodoret, the most religious Bishop of Cyrus: The epistle of the most holy Archbishop, the lord Leo, agrees with the faith established at Nice by the holy and blessed fathers, and with the symbol of faith expounded at Constantinople by the hundred and fifty, and with the epistles of the blessed Cyril. And accepting it, I have subscribed the said epistle."' And thus all in succession: "The epistle corresponds," "the epistle is consonant," the epistle agrees in sense," and the like. After such great and very severe scrutiny in comparing it with former holy Councils, and a full conviction of the correctness of the meaning, and not merely because it was the epistle of the Pope, they cried aloud, ungrudgingly, the exclamation on which his Holiness now vaunts himself: But if his Holiness had sent us statements concordant and in unison with the seven holy

Ecumenical Councils, instead of boasting of the piety of his predecessors lauded by our predecessors and fathers in an Ecumenical Council, he might justly have gloried in his own orthodoxy, declaring his own goodness instead of that of his fathers. Therefore let his Holiness be assured, that if, even now, he will write us such things as two hundred fathers on investigation and inquiry shall find consonant and agreeing with the said former Councils, then, we say, he shall hear from us sinners today, not only, "Peter has so spoken," or anything of like honor, but this also, "Let the holy hand be kissed which has wiped away the tears of the Catholic Church."

16. And surely we have a right to expect from the prudent forethought of his Holiness, a work so worthy the true successor of St. Peter, of Leo I, and also of Leo III, who for security of the orthodox faith engraved the divine Creed unaltered upon imperishable plates—a work which will unite the churches of the West to the holy Catholic Church, in which the canonical chief seat of his Holiness, and the seats of all the Bishops of the West remain empty and ready to be occupied. For the Catholic Church, awaiting the conversion of the shepherds who have fallen off from her with their flocks, does not separate in name only, those who have been privily introduced to the rulership by the action of others, thus making little of the Priesthood. But we are expecting the "word of consolation," and hope that he, as wrote St. Basil to St. Ambrose, Bishop of Milan (Epis. b6), will "tread again the ancient footprints of the fathers." Not without great astonishment have we read

the said Encyclical letter to the Easterns, in which we see with deep grief of soul his Holiness, famed for prudence, speaking like his predecessors in schism, words that urge upon us the adulteration of our pure holy Creed, on which the Ecumenical Councils have set their seal; and doing violence to the sacred Liturgies, whose heavenly structure alone, and the names of those who framed them, and their tone of reverend antiquity, and the stamp that was placed upon them by the Seventh Ecumenical Synod (Act vi.), should have paralyzed him, and made him to turn aside the sacrilegious and all-daring hand that has thus smitten the King of Glory. From these things we estimate into what an unspeakable labyrinth of wrong and incorrigible sin of revolution the papacy has thrown even the wiser and more godly Bishops of the Roman Church, so that, in order to preserve the innocent, and therefore valued vicarial dignity, as well as the despotic primacy and the things depending upon it, they know no other means save to insult the most divine and sacred things, daring everything for that one end. Clothing themselves, in words, with pious reverence for "the most venerable antiquity" (p. xi. 1.16), in reality there remains, within, the innovating temper; and yet his Holiness really bears hard upon himself when he says that we "must cast from us everything that has crept in among us since the Separation,"(!) while he and his have spread the poison of their innovation even into the Supper of our LORD. His Holiness evidently takes it for granted that in the Orthodox Church the same thing has happened which he is conscious has happened in the Church of Rome since the rise of the Papacy: to wit, a sweeping change in all the Mysteries, and corruption from scholastic subtleties, a reliance on which must suffice as an equivalent for our sacred Liturgies and Mysteries and doctrines: yet all the while, forsooth, reverencing our "venerable antiquity," and all this by a condescension entirely Apostolic! — "without," as he says, "troubling us by any harsh conditions"! From such ignorance of the Apostolic and Catholic food on which we live emanates another sententious declaration of his (p. vii. 1. 22): "It is not possible that unity of doctrine and sacred observance should be preserved among you," paradoxically ascribing to us the very misfortune from which he suffers at home; just as Pope Leo IX wrote to the blessed Michael Cerularius, accusing the Greeks of changing the Creed of the Catholic Church, without blushing either for his own honor or for the truth of history. We are persuaded that if his Holiness will call to mind ecclesiastical archaeology and history, the doctrine of the holy Fathers and the old Liturgies of France and Spain, and the Sacramentary of the ancient Roman Church, he will be struck with surprise on finding how many other monstrous daughters, now living, the Papacy has brought forth in the West: while Orthodoxy, with us, has preserved the Catholic Church as an incorruptible bride for her Bridegroom, although we have no temporal power, nor, as his Holiness says, any sacred "observances," but by the sole tie of love and affection to a common Mother are bound together in the unity of a faith sealed with the *seven seals of the Spirit* (Rev. v. 1), and by the seven Ecumenical Councils, and in obedience to the Truth. He will find, also, how many modern papistical doctrines and mysteries must be rejected as "commandments of men" in order that the Church of the West, which has introduced all sorts of novelties, may be changed back again to the immutable Catholic Orthodox faith of our common fathers. As his Holiness recognizes our common zeal in this faith, when he says (p. viii. l.30), "let us take heed to the doctrine preserved by our forefathers," so he does well in instructing us (l. 31) to follow the old pontiffs and the faithful of the Eastern Metropolitans. What these thought of the doctrinal fidelity of the Archbishops of the elder Rome, and what idea we ought to have of them in the Orthodox Church, and in what manner we ought to receive their teachings, they have synodically given us an example (§ 15), and the sublime Basil has well interpreted it (§ 7). As to the supremacy, since we are not setting forth a treatise, let the same great Basil present the matter in a few words, "I preferred to address myself to Him who is Head over them."

17. From all this, every one nourished in sound Catholic doctrine, particularly his Holiness, must draw the conclusion, how impious and anti-synodical it is to attempt the alteration of our doctrine and liturgies and other divine offices which are, and are proved to be, coeval with the preaching of Christianity: for which reason reverence was always bestowed on them, and they were confided in as pure even by the old orthodox Popes themselves, to whom these things were an inheritance in common with ourselves. How becoming and holy would be the mending of the innovations, the time

of whose entrance in the Church of Rome we know in each case; for our illustrious fathers have testified from time to time against each novelty. But there are other reasons which should incline his Holiness to this change. First, because those things that are ours were once venerable to the Westerns, as having the same divine Offices and confessing the same Creed; but the novelties were not known to our Fathers, nor could they be shown in the writings of the orthodox Western Fathers, nor as having their origin either in antiquity or catholicity. Moreover, neither Patriarchs nor Councils could then have introduced novelties amongst us, because the protector of religion is the very body of the Church, even the people themselves, who desire their religious worship to be ever unchanged and of the same kind as that of their fathers: for as, after the Schism, many of the Popes and Latinizing Patriarchs made attempts that came to nothing even in the Western Church; and as, from time to time, either by fair means or foul, the Popes have commanded novelties for the sake of expediency (as they have explained to our fathers, although they were thus dismembering the Body of Christ): so now again the Pope, for the sake of a truly divine and most just expediency, forsooth (not mending the nets, but himself rending the garment of the Savior), dares to oppose the venerable things of antiquity, — things well fitted to preserve religion, as his Holiness confesses (p. xi. 1.16), and which he himself honors, as he says (lib. 1.16), together with his predecessors, for he repeats that memorable expression of one of those blessed predecessors (Celestine, writing to the third

Ecumenical Council): "Let novelty cease to attack antiquity." And let the Catholic Church enjoy this benefit from this so far blameless declaration of the Popes. It must by all means be confessed, that in such his attempt, even though Pius IX be eminent for wisdom and piety, and, as he says, for zeal after Christian unity in the Catholic Church, he will meet, within and without, with difficulties and toils. And here we must put his Holiness in mind, if he will excuse our boldness, of that portion of his letter (p. viii. L.32), "That in things which relate to the confession of our divine religion, nothing is to be feared, when we look to the glory of Christ, and the reward which awaits us in eternal life." It is incumbent on his Holiness to show before God and man, that, as prime mover of the counsel which pleases God, so is he a willing protector of the ill-treated evangelical and synodical truth, even to the sacrifice of his own interests, according to the Prophet (Is. lx. 17), A ruler in peace and a bishop in righteousness. So be it! But until there be this desired returning of the apostate Churches to the body of the One, Holy, Catholic, and Apostolic Church, of which Christ is the Head (Eph. iv. 15), and each of us "members in particular," all advice proceeding from them, and every officious exhortation tending to the dissolution of our pure faith handed down from the Fathers is condemned, as it ought to be, synodically, not only as suspicious and to be eschewed, but as impious and soul-destroying: and in this category, among the first we place the said Encyclical to the Easterns from Pope Pius IX, Bishop of the elder Rome; and such we proclaim it to be in the Catholic Church.

18. Wherefore, beloved brethren and fellow-ministers of our mediocrity, as always, so also now, particularly on this occasion of the publication of the said Encyclical, we hold it to be our inexorable duty, in accordance with our patriarchal and synodical responsibility, in order that none may be lost to the divine fold of the Catholic Orthodox Church, the most holy Mother of us all, to encourage each other, and to urge you that, reminding one another of the words and exhortations of St. Paul to our holy predecessors when he summoned them to Ephesus, we reiterate to each other: *take heed, therefore, unto yourselves, and to all the flock, over the which the Holy Spirit hath made you overseers, to feed the Church of God, which He hath purchased with His own Blood. For know this, that after my departing shall grievous wolves enter in among you not sparing the flock. Also of your own selves shall men arise, speaking perverse things, to draw away disciples after them. Therefore, watch.* (Acts xx.28-31.) Then our predecessors and Fathers, hearing this divine charge, wept sore, and falling upon his neck, kissed him. Come, then, and let us, brethren, hearing him admonishing us with tears, fall in spirit, lamenting, upon his neck, and, kissing him, comfort him by our own firm assurance, that no one shall separate us from the love of Christ, no one mislead us from evangelical doctrine, no one entice us from the safe path of our fathers, as none was able to deceive them, by any degree of zeal which they manifested, who from time to time were raised up for this purpose by the tempter: so that at last we shall hear from the Master: Well done, good and faithful servant, receiving the end of our faith, even the

salvation of our souls, and of the reasonable flock over whom the Holy Spirit has made us shepherds.

19. This Apostolic charge and exhortation we have quoted for your sake, and address it to all the Orthodox congregation, wherever they be found settled on the earth, to the Priests and Abbots, to the Deacons and Monks, in a word, to all the Clergy and godly People, the rulers and the ruled, the rich and the poor, to parents and children, to teachers and scholars, to the educated and uneducated, to masters and servants, that we all, supporting and counseling each other, may be able to stand against the wiles of the devil. For thus St. Peter the Apostle exhorts us (1 Pet.): *Be sober, be vigilant because your adversary the devil, as a roaring lion walketh about, seeking whom he may devour.* Whom resist, steadfast in the faith.

20. For our faith, brethren, is not of men nor by man, but by revelation of Jesus Christ, which the divine Apostles preached, the holy Ecumenical Councils confirmed, the greatest and wisest teachers of the world handed down in succession, and the shed blood of the holy martyrs ratified. Let us hold fast to the confession which we have received unadulterated from such men, turning away from every novelty as a suggestion of the devil. He that accepts a novelty reproaches with deficiency the preached Orthodox Faith. But that Faith has long ago been sealed in completeness, not to admit of diminution or increase, or any change whatever; and he who dares to do, or advise, or think of such a thing has already denied the faith of Christ, has already of his own accord been struck with an eternal anathema, for

blaspheming the Holy Spirit as not having spoken fully in the Scriptures and through the Ecumenical Councils. This fearful anathema, brethren and sons beloved in Christ, we do not pronounce today, but our Savior first pronounced it (Matt. xii. 32): *Whosoever speaketh against the Holy Spirit, it shall not be forgiven him, neither in this world, neither in the world to come.* St. Paul pronounced the same anathema (Gal. i. 6): *I marvel that ye are so soon removed from Him that called you into the grace of Christ, unto another Gospel: which is not another; but there be some that trouble you, and would pervert the Gospel of Christ. But though we, or an angel from heaven, preach any other gospel unto you, than that which we have preached unto you, let him be accursed.* This same anathema the Seven Ecumenical Councils and the whole choir of God-serving fathers pronounced. All, therefore, innovating, either by heresy or schism, have voluntarily clothed themselves, according to the Psalm (cix. 18), *with a curse as with a garment,* whether they be Popes, or Patriarchs, or Clergy, or Laity; nay, if any one, though an angel from heaven, preach any other Gospel unto you than that ye have received, let him be accursed. Thus our wise fathers, obedient to the soul-saving words of St. Paul, were established firm and steadfast in the faith handed down unbrokenly to them, and preserved it unchanged and uncontaminated in the midst of so many heresies, and have delivered it to us pure and undefiled, as it came pure from the mouth of the first servants of the Word. Let us, too, thus wise, transmit it, pure as we have received it, to coming generations, altering nothing, that they may be, as we are, full of confidence, and with nothing to be ashamed of when speaking of the faith of their forefathers.

21. Therefore, brethren, and sons beloved in the LORD, *having purified your souls in obeying the truth* (1 Pet. i. 22), *let us give the more earnest heed to the things which we have heard, lest at any time we should let them slip* (Heb. ii. 1.). The faith and confession we have received is not one to be ashamed of, being taught in the Gospel from the mouth of our LORD, witnessed by the holy Apostles, by the seven sacred Ecumenical Councils, preached throughout the world, witnessed to by its very enemies, who, before they apostatized from orthodoxy to heresies, themselves held this same faith, or at least their fathers and fathers' fathers thus held it. It is witnessed to by continuous history, as triumphing over all the heresies which have persecuted or now persecute it, as ye see even to this day. The succession of our holy divine fathers and predecessors beginning from the Apostles, and those whom the Apostles appointed their successors, to this day, forming one unbroken chain, and joining hand to hand, keep fast the sacred enclosure of which the door is Christ, in which all the orthodox Flock is fed in the fertile pastures of the mystical Eden, and not in the pathless and rugged wilderness, as his Holiness supposes (p. 7.1.12). Our Church holds the infallible and genuine deposit of the Holy Scriptures, of the Old Testament a true and perfect version, of the New the divine original itself. The rites of the sacred Mysteries, and especially those of the Divine Liturgy, are the same glorious and heartquickening rites, handed down from the Apostles. No nation,

no Christian communion, can boast of such Liturgies as those of James, Basil, Chrysostom. The august Ecumenical Councils, those seven pillars of the house of Wisdom, were organized in it and among us. This, our Church, holds the originals of their sacred definitions. The Chief Pastors in it, and the honorable Presbytery, and the monastic Order, preserve the primitive and pure dignity of the first ages of Christianity, in opinions, in polity, and even in the simplicity of their vestments. Yes! Verily, "grievous wolves" have constantly attacked this holy fold, and are attacking it now, as we see for ourselves, according to the prediction of the Apostle, which shows that the true lambs of the great Shepherd are folded in it; but that Church has sung and shall sing forever: *They compassed me about; yea, they compassed me about: but in the name of the Lord I will destroy them* (Ps. cxviii. 11). Let us add one reflection, a painful one indeed, but useful in order to manifest and confirm the truth of our words: All Christian nations whatsoever that are today seen calling upon the Name of Christ (not excepting either the West generally, or Rome herself, as we prove by the catalogue of her earliest Popes), were taught the true faith in Christ by our holy predecessors and fathers; and yet afterwards deceitful men, many of whom were shepherds, and chief shepherds too, of those nations, by wretched sophistries and heretical opinions dared to defile, alas! the orthodoxy of those nations, as veracious history informs us, and as St. Paul predicted.

22. Therefore, brethren, and ye our spiritual children, we acknowledge how great the favor and grace

which God has bestowed upon our Orthodox Faith, and on His One, Holy, Catholic, and Apostolic Church, which, like a mother who is unsuspected of her husband, nourishes us as children of whom she is not ashamed, and who are excusable in our high-toned boldness concerning the hope that is in us. But what shall we sinners render to the LORD for all that He hath bestowed upon us? Our bounteous LORD and God, who hath redeemed us by his own Blood, requires nothing else of us but the devotion of our whole soul and heart to the blameless, holy faith of our fathers, and love and affection to the Orthodox Church, which has regenerated us not with a novel sprinkling, but with the divine washing of Apostolic Baptism. She it is that nourishes us, according to the eternal covenant of our Savior, with His own precious Body, and abundantly, as a true Mother, gives us to drink of that precious Blood poured out for us and for the salvation of the world. Let us then encompass her in spirit, as the young their parent bird, wherever on earth we find ourselves, in the north or south, or east, or west. Let us fix our eyes and thoughts upon her divine countenance and her most glorious beauty. Let us take hold with both our hands on her shining robe which the Bridegroom, "altogether lovely," has with His own undefiled hands thrown around her, when He redeemed her from the bondage of error, and adorned her as an eternal Bride for Himself. Let us feel in our own souls the mutual grief of the children-loving mother and the mother-loving children, when it is seen that men of wolfish minds and making gain of souls are zealous in plotting how they may lead her captive, or tear the lambs from their mothers. Let us, Clergy as well as Laity, cherish this feeling most intensely now, when the unseen adversary of our salvation, combining his fraudful arts (p. xi. 1. 2-25), employs such powerful instrumentalities, and walketh about everywhere, as saith St. Peter, *seeking whom he may devour*; and when in this way, in which we walk peacefully and innocently, he sets his deceitful snares.

23. Now, the God of peace, "that brought again from the dead that great Shepherd of the sheep," *He that keepeth Israel, who shall neither slumber nor sleep, keep your hearts and minds, and direct your ways to every good work*. Peace and joy be with you in the LORD.

May 1848, Indiction 6.

+ ANTHIMOS, Archbishop of Constantinople, new Rome, and Ecumenical.

+ HIEROTHEUS, Patriarch of Alexandria and of all Egypt.

+ METHODIOS, Patriarch of the great City of God, Antioch, and of all Anatolia.

+ CYRIL, Patriarch of Jerusalem and of all Palestine.

APPENDIX C

The *Tomus* of 1285

The official statement, or **Tomus,** *of the Ortho-dox Council of Blachernae held in 1285. This council represents the* official *position of the Orthodox Church concerning the* **Filioque.**

On July 6, 1274 at the Council of Lyons, representa-tives of the Roman emperor and representatives of the pope announced the union of the Orthodox and Roman Catholic Churches. As with most reunion attempts, this was motivated primarily by political concerns. Ecu-menical Patriarch Joseph abdicated upon the return of the imperial legates in 1275. John Beccus was elected to succeed him. Beccus became the emperor's "point-man" on the issue and was charged with the task of gaining Church-wide acceptance of the union.

Beccus' career reads like the script to a soap opera. Fiercely anti-Latin, he was imprisoned by the emperor for his inflammatory rhetoric. While in prison, he ap-parently "converted" to the Roman Catholic under-standing of the *Filioque*. Once enthroned as patriarch, he became the primary proponent of Roman Catholic-Orthodox union and of the *Filioque* in the Eastern Ro-man Empire.

In spite of Beccus' best efforts, however, the Church at large accepted neither the union nor the *Filioque*. Furthermore, the cause for union was complicated by papal insistence that the *Filioque* actually be used in Constantinople (as opposed to merely being accepted) and that Orthodox clergy sign an oath acknowledging papal primacy. Papadakis observes:

> In a very real sense, [Pope] Nicholas' demands, which threatened the integrity of Byzantine custom, were as unwelcome to the unionists as to the Orthodox. Both agreed it was too much to request the recitation of the *Filioque* of everyone. It was one thing for the emperor to do so (it was public knowledge that he had professed it at Lyons through his ambassadors), and another for the entire church suddenly to begin chanting it in the liturgy. In short, the bishops, and many of those who had opposed the union, soon realized their fears had come true. Not surprisingly, [Emperor] Michael was forced to fabricate episcopal signatures in his attempt to convince Pope Nicholas of his efforts to force the union on his subjects.[1]

In 1282, Emperor Michael was succeeded by his son Andronicus, who quickly reversed his father's unionist policy. He restored the former patriarch, Joseph, to the throne, and Joseph issued depositions and suspensions to Beccus and other clergy who had supported the Union of Lyons. Beccus signed a solemn declaration repu-

---

[1]Aristides Papadakis, *Crisis in Byzantium: The Filioque Controversy in the Patriarchate of Gregory II of Cyprus (1283-1289)* (Crestwood, NY: SVS Press, 1997), p.26.

diating his support for the *Filioque* and union with Rome. It was not long, however, before Beccus repudiated his repudiation.

Upon the Death of Patriarch Joseph in March of 1283, Gregory II of Cyprus ascended the patriarchal throne. Gregory was responsible for drawing up the *Tomus,* or official statement, of the Council of Blachernae in 1285. It is occasionally argued that the Orthodox Church has never *officially* condemned the *Filioque* as a heresy. This is manifestly not true. In condemning the unionist theology of John Beccus, the Council specifically and irrevocably condemned the Latin doctrine of the *Filioque* as a heresy.

Exposition of the Tomus of Faith Against Beccus[2]

By the most holy and ecumenical patriarch, Lord Gregory of Cyprus, who was attacked by certain individuals, and for whom this vigorous reply was given...[3]

It is, likewise, commendable, and truly[4] salutary, and the work of superior planning to attend to the future safety of the Church and, in every way, to secure its stability so that if someone hateful to God should again attempt to disturb it he will be shown to be acting

[2]The translation of this text is taken from Aristides Papadakis, *Crisis in Byzantium,* pp. 212-229, and is reprinted with the permission of St. Vladimir's Seminary Press. All footnotes from this point forward are from Papadakis' edition.

[3]For the other longer superscriptions, see Laurent, *Regestes,* no. 1490, p. 282.

[4]Paris. Gr. 1301. Fol. 88ᵛ: ὄντως; omitted by Banduri (p. 943).

in vain, because he will be repelled by the unshakable words of our faith. This could be accomplished satisfactorily if we do two things. We should first define our belief dearly [clearly? — C.C.], that is, the Orthodox faith, and raise it as a permanent monument to our sublime faith; seen, thus, from a distance — being visible to all — it will attract to itself the spiritual eyes of everyone. Secondly we must make this evil, (fol. 89ʳ) destructive and alien teaching known, so that when this has been exposed we will all turn away from it and despise it and quickly escape from danger.

Accordingly, the faith which we acknowledge and believe [235C-D] in our heart is as follows. We believe as we have been taught from the beginning and from the Fathers. We have been taught and we believe in one God, the Father almighty, creator of heaven and earth, and of all things visible and invisible, who, being without principle (ἄναρχος), unbegotten, and without cause, is the natural principle and cause of the Son and of the Spirit. We also believe in His only begotten Son, who, being consubstantial with Him, was begotten eternally and without change from Him, through whom all things were made.[5] We believe in the all-Holy Spirit, which proceeds from the same Father, which, with the Father and the Son together, is worshipped as co-eternal, co-equal, co-essential, co-equal in glory, and as joint-creator of the world. We believe that the only begotten (fol. 89ᵛ) Word of the supersubstantial and life-

[5]See John of Damascus, De fide orthodoxa, B. Kotter (ed.), Die Schriften des Johannes von Damaskos, II (Patristische Texte und Studien, 12; Berlin, 1973), 19-20, 23 (= PG 94.809-11, 816C).

giving Trinity came down from heaven for us men and for our salvation, was incarnate by the Holy Spirit and the Virgin Mary and became man; that is, He became prefect man while remaining God and in no way altered or transformed the divine nature by His contact with the flesh, but assumed humanity without change. And He, who is passionless according to His divine nature, suffered the passion and the cross and, on the third day, rose from the dead and ascended into heaven and sat at the right hand of God the Father. We believe in accordance with God, holy tradition and teaching [236A-B] in one holy, catholic, and apostolic Church. We acknowledge one baptism for the remission of sins; we look for the resurrection of the dead, and the life of the age to come.

Additionally, we acknowledge a single hypostasis of the incarnate Word, and we believe the same Christ to be one, and we proclaim and know Him after the Incarnation, as redeeming with two natures, (fol. 90ʳ) from which, and in which, and which He is. Consequently, we believe in two energies and two wills of the same Christ, each nature having its own will and its own saving action. We venerate, but not[6] absolutely and without adoration, the holy and sacred images of Christ, of the immaculate Mother of God, and of all the saints, because the honor we show them passes over to the original. We reject the recently established union [of Lyons] which provoked God's hostility toward us.[7] For

---

[6]Paris. Gr. 1301, fol. 90ʳ: ἀλλ' οὐ; Banduri (p. 943): καὶ οὐ.

[7]Cf. Rom. 8:7 "For, the mind that is set on the flesh is hostile to God."

this union divided and ravaged the Church, under the pretense of harmless accommodation, persuading it, by their stupidity and deception, to establish their glory, but not God's,[8] and to turn from Orthodoxy and the sound teaching of the Fathers, and to fall down the precipice of heresy and blasphemy.[9] We also render void their dangerous doctrine concerning the procession of the Holy Spirit. (fol. 90v) We have been taught from God, the Word Himself, that the all-Holy Spirit proceeds from the Father; and we confess that it has its existence from the Father, and that it prides itself — exactly as the [236C-D] Son Himself does — in the fact that the same [Father] is essentially the cause of its being. And we know and believe that the Son is from the Father, being enriched in having the Father as His cause and natural principle, and in being consubstantial and of one nature with the Spirit, which is from the Father. Even so, He is not, either separately or with the Father, the cause of the Spirit; for the all-Holy Spirit's existence is not "through the Son" and "from the Son" as they

[8]Rom. 10:3: "For, being ignorant of the righteousness that comes from God, and seeking to establish their own, they did not submit to God's righteousness."

[9]The word "blasphemy" is used repeatedly by Gregory to describe Beccus' doctrine concerning the procession of the Spirit. To be sure, the deeply biblical nuance of the word in Scripture and in patristic literature did not escape him. In the New Testament, the word indicates violation of the power and majesty of God (Mark 2:7; Luke 5:21). In the early patristic period, opposing theological views were stigmatized as blasphemy. See especially G. Kittel (ed.), *Theological Dictionary of the New Testament*, I (Grand Rapids-London, 1964), 621-25.

who hasten toward their destruction and separation from God understand and teach.[10] We shun and cut off from our communion those who do not correctly uphold the sound faith but blaspheme blatantly, and think and speak perversely[11] and perpetuate what is most alarming[12] and unbearable to hear...

3. To the same, who say that the Father is, through the Son, the cause of the Spirit, and who cannot conceive [240A-B] the Father as the cause of the hypostasis of the Spirit—giving it existence and being—except through the Son; thus according to them the Son is united to the Father as a joint-cause and contributor of the Spirit's existence. This, they say, is supported by the phrase of Saint John of Damascus, "the Father is the projector through the Son of the manifesting Spirit."[13] This, however, can never mean what they say, inasmuch as it clearly denotes the manifestation—through the intermediary of the Son—of the Spirit, whose existence is from the Father.[14] For the same John of Damas-

---

[10]Psalm 73:27: "For lo, those who are far from thee shall perish; thou dost put and end to those who are false to thee."

[11]Acts 20:30: "And from among your own selves will arise men speaking perverse things, to draw away the disciples after them."

[12]Paris. gr. 1301, fol. 90ᵛ: δεινότατον; Banduri (p. 944): δεινοτάτης.

[13]John of Damascus, *De fide orthodoxa*, in Kotter, *Die Schriften des Johannes von Damaskos* II, 36 (=PG94.849B). "He Himself [the Father], then, is mind, the depth of reason, begetter of the Word, and, through the Word, projector of the manifesting Spirit."

[14]This is the sentence which the commission (set up after June 1289) decided to excise from the text. This decision, however, was

cus would not have said—in the exact same chapter—
that the only cause in the Trinity is God the Father, thus
denying, by the use of the word "only," the causative
principle to the remaining two hypostases.[15] Nor would
he have, again, said elsewhere, "and we speak, likewise,
of the Holy Spirit as the 'Spirit of the Son,' yet we do
not speak of the Spirit as from the Son."[16] For both of
these views to be true is impossible (fol. 95^v). To those
who have not accepted the interpretation given to these
testimonia by the fathers, but, on the contrary, perceive
them in a manner altogether forbidden by them, we
pronounce the above recorded resolution and judgment, we cut them off from the membership of the Orthodox, and we banish them from the flock of the
Church of God.

4. To the same, who affirm that the Paraclete, which
is from the Father, has its existence through the Son and
from the Son, and who again propose as proof the
phrase "the Spirit exists through the Son and from the
Son." In certain texts [of the Fathers], the phrase denotes the [240C-D] Spirit's shining forth and manifestation. Indeed, the very Paraclete shines from and is
manifest eternally through the Son, in the same way
that light shines forth and is manifest through the intermediary of the sun's rays; it further denotes the be-
stowing, giving, and sending of the Spirit to us. It does

probably not carried out, for the manuscript tradition has preserved the text in its original form only, without any suppression.

[15]John of Damascus, *De fide orthodoxa*, in Kotter, *Die Schriften
des Johannes von Damaskos* II, 36 (=PG94.849B).

[16]Ibid., 30 (=PG 94-832B).

not, however, mean that it subsists through the Son and from the Son, and that it receives its being through Him and from Him. For this would[17] mean that the Spirit has the Son as cause and source (exactly as it has the Father), not to say that it has its cause and source more so from the Son than from the Father; for it is said that that from which existence is derived likewise is believed to enrich the source and to be the cause of being. (fol. 96ʳ) To those who believe and say such things, we pronounce the above resolution and judgment, we cut them off from the membership of the Orthodox, and we banish them from the flock of the Church of God.

5. To the same, who say that the preposition "through" everywhere in theology is identical to the preposition "from" and, as a result, maintain that there is no difference in saying that the Spirit proceeds "through the Son" from saying that it proceeds "from the Son" — whence, undoubtedly, the origin of their idea that the existence and essence of the Spirit is from the Son. And they either infer a double or a single procession of origin, and join the Son to the Father according to this explanation of "cause," both of which are beyond all blasphemy. For there is no other hypostasis in the Trinity except the Father's, from which the existence and essence of the consubstantial [Son and Holy Spirit] is derived. According [241A-B] to the common mind of the Church and the aforementioned saints, the Father is the foundation and the source of the Son and the Spirit, the only source of divinity, and the only cause. If, in

---

[17]Paris. Gr. 1301, fol. 95ᵛ: οὕτω; Banduri (p. 946): ὄντως.

fact, it is also said by some of the saints that the Spirit proceeds "through the Son," (fol. 96^v) what is meant here is the eternal manifestation of the Spirit by the Son, not the purely [personal] emanation into being of the Spirit, which has its existence from the Father.[18] Otherwise, this would deprive the Father from being the only cause and the only source of divinity, and would expose the theologian [Gregory of Nazianzus] who says "everything the Father is said to possess, the Son, likewise, possesses except causality"[19] as a dishonest theologian. To those who speak thus, we pronounce the above-recorded resolution and judgment, we cut them off from the membership of the Orthodox, and we banish them from the flock of the Church of God.

6. To the same, who contend that the unique essence and divinity of the Father and the Son is the cause of the Spirit's existence—an idea which no one who has ever had it in his mind has either expressed or considered making public. For the common essence and nature is not the cause of the hypostasis; nor does this common essence ever generate or project that which is undivided; on the other hand, the essence which is accompanied by individual characteristics does, and this, according to the great Maximus, denotes the hyposta-

---

[18]The sentence which the monk Mark chose to elaborate upon in his commentary, the synod of bishops later demanded a retraction of his confusing explanation. See *Crisis*, Chapter 7.

[19]Gregory of Nazianzus, *Oratio* 34, PG 36.252A; cf. also Mouzalon's use and explanation of this proof-text, in PG 142.293A-B.

sis.[20] But also, according to the great Basil, because he too defines the hypostasis as that (fol. 97r) which describes and brings to mind what in each thing is common, and which cannot be described by means of individual characteristics which appear in it.[21] Because of this, the indivisible essence always projects something indivisible (or generates the indivisible [241C-D] that generates),[22] in order that the created may be [simultaneously] the projector as well as the projected; the essence of the Father and the Son, however, is one, and is not, on the whole, indivisible.[23] To these, who absurdly blaspheme thus, we pronounce the above-recorded resolution and judgment, we cut them off from the membership of the Orthodox, and we banish them from the flock of the Church of God.

7. To the same, who teach that the Father and the Son—not as two principles and two causes—share in the causality of the Spirit, and that the Son is as much a participant with the Father as is implied in the preposition "through." According to the distinction and strength of these prepositions, they introduce a distinction in the Spirit's cause, with the result that sometimes they believe and say that the Father is cause, and some-

[20]Cf. Maximus the Confessor, *Letter 7: To John the Presbyter*, PG 91.436A.

[21]Basil, *locus incognitus*.

[22]Banduri (p. 946) omits the clause in parentheses: ἤ γεννᾷ καὶ δεῖ τὸ γεννῶν ἄτομον (Paris. Gr. 1301, fol. 97ʳ); other manuscripts substitute δὴ for the word δεῖ.

[23]On this section, cf. John of Damascus, *De fide orthodoxa*, in Kotter, *die Schriften des Johannes von Damaskos*, II, 27 (=PG 94.825A-B).

times the Son. This being so, they introduce a plurality and a multitude of causes in the procession of the Spirit, even though this was prohibited on countless occasions. (fol. 97ᵛ) As such, we pronounce the above-recorded resolution and judgment, we cut them off from the membership of the Orthodox, and we banish them from the flock of the Church of God.

8. To the same, who stoutly maintain that the Father by virtue of the nature—not by virtue of the hypostasis—is the Holy Spirit's cause; the result is that they necessarily proclaim the Son as a cause of the Spirit, since the Son has the same nature as the Father. At the same time, they fail to see the absurdity that results from this. [242A-B] For it is necessary first[24] that the Spirit be the cause of someone, for the simple reason that it has the same nature as the Father. Secondly, the number of the cause increases, since as many hypostases as share in nature must, likewise, share in causality. Thirdly, the common essence and nature is transformed into the cause of the hypostasis, which all logic—and, along with this, nature itself—prohibits. (fol. 98ʳ) To these, who believe in such things strange and alien to truth, we pronounce the above-recorded resolution and judgment, we cut them off from the membership of the Orthodox, and we banish them from the flock of the Church of God.

9. To the same, who state that, in reference to the creation of the world, the phrase "through the Son" de-

---

[24]Paris. Gr. 1301, fol. 97v: πρῶτα; Banduri (p. 947): ἄρα τά.

notes the immediate cause,[25] as well as the fact that it denies the Son the right to be creator and cause of things made "through Him." That is to say, in theology proper [the study of the Trinity in itself], even if the Father is called the initial cause of the Son and the Spirit, He is also, "through the Son," the cause of the Spirit. Accordingly, the Son cannot be separated from the Father in the procession of the Spirit. By saying such things, they irrationally join the Son to the Father in the causation of the Spirit. In reality, even if the Son, like the Father, is creator of all things made "through Him," it does not follow that He is also the Spirit's cause, because the Father is the projector of the Spirit through Him; nor, again, does it follow that, because the Father is the Spirit's projector "through[26] the Son," He is, through Him, the cause of the Spirit. For the formula "through the Son" here denotes the manifestation and illumination [of the Spirit by the Son], and not the emanation [242C-D] of the Sprit into being. If this was not so, it would be difficult, indeed even to enumerate the theological absurdities that follow. To these, who irrationally express such views, and ascribe them to the writings of the saints, and from these stir up a multitude of blasphemies, we pronounce the above- (fol. 98ᵛ) recorded resolution and judgment, we cut them off from the membership of the Orthodox, and we banish them from the flock of the Church of God...

[25]Immediate or primordial cause: προκαταρκτικὴ αἰτία; cf. Basil, *On the Holy Spirit*, PG 31.136B.

[26]Paris. Gr. 1301, fol. 98r: διὰ τοῦ; Banduri (p. 947): δι' αὐτοῦ.

11. To the same, who do not receive the writings of the saints in the correct manner intended by the Church, nor do they honor what appears to be the closest [interpretation] according to the patristic[27] traditions and the common beliefs about God and things divine, but distort[28] the meaning of these writings so as to set them at variance with the prescribed dogmas, or adhere to the mere word and, from this, bring forth strange doctrine, we pronounce the above-recorded resolution and judgment, we cut them off from the membership of the Orthodox, and we banish them from the flock of the Church of God...

For where have the God-bearing Fathers said that God the Father is, through the Son, the cause of the Spirit? Where do they say that the Paraclete has its existence from the Son and though the Son? Again, where do they say that the same Paraclete has its existence from the Father and from the Son? In what text do they teach that the one essence and divinity of the Father and the Son is the cause of the Holy Spirit's existence? Who, and in which of his works, ever prohibited anyone from saying that the hypostasis of the Father is the unique cause of being of the Son and the Spirit? Who among those who believe that the Father is the cause of the Spirit has taught that this is by virtue of the nature,

[27]Paris. Gr. 1301, fol. 99ʳ: πατρικάς; Banduri (p. 947): πνευματικάς.

[28]Paris. Gr. 1301, fol. 99ʳ: ἐκβιάζουσι; Banduri (p. 947) ἐκβιβάζουσιν.

not by[29] virtue of the hypostasis? And who has failed to maintain this as (fol. 100^r) the characteristic that distinguishes the Father from the other two hypostases? Finally, who says that those other teachings, about which he has lied by insulting the Fathers, belong to the Fathers? He abstains from neither evil. For at some places he alters their own words, and, even when he uses the words without distortion, he does not adhere to their true meaning. Neither does he look at the aim that the author had in mind, but arrogantly passes over the purpose and the desire, and even the express intent of the author's statement, and adheres to the word and, having obtained the shadow instead of the body, composes books. And this is like saying that [244 A-B] he twists ropes of sand and builds houses therefrom to make I do not know what, unless it is a monument and a memorial—the former, an advertisement of his folly the latter, a declaration of the struggle he undertook against his own salvation. This being so, we condemn the doctrines themselves together with their authors, and judge that their memory, like the expelled, be eliminated from the Church with a resounding noise...

Thus, we define our position very clearly for everyone, should any individual—living now or in the future—ever dare to revive that act which has been wisely abolished, or attempt to impose doctrines on our Church which have been already profitably condemned, or suggest them either secretly and[30] mali-

---

[29]Banduri (p. 948) adds ἀλλά; the word, which is unnecessary, is not found in Paris. Gr. 1301, fol. 99^v.

[30]Paris. Gr. 1301, fol. 101^r: καὶ; Banduri (p. 948): ἤ.

ciously, or introduce a proposal in favor of believing or approving these doctrines, or strive for their free acceptance among us, and thus scorn the genuine doctrines of the early Church and its present decrees against the spurious and alien and, indeed, against the accommodation and act by which they crept into the Church to its detriment. This Beccus, and anyone who agrees ever to receive those members of the Roman Church who remain intransigent concerning those doctrines for which they were from the beginning accused by our Church and for which the schism occurred, and who agree to receive them (fol. 101v) more openly than we were accustomed, that is, prior to this misleading accommodation and worthless union [of Lyons] hostile to the good—this man, besides expelling him from the Church, cutting him off, and removing him from the assembly and society of the faithful, we subject to the terrible penalty of anathema. For he should not even be forgiven [245 A-B] by men, he who did not learn not to dare such things (after such an experience of the preceding evil, or after the recent condemnation), and who did not understand not to contrive against the accepted formulations of the Fathers, nor to remain[31] forever a disciple and subject of the Church.

And we proclaim and do these things, as we said, for the sake of remaining spiritually unharmed, for the mutual benefit of everyone, for those who now belong to our devout Church, and for those who after this shall

[31]Paris. Gr. 1301, fol. 101ᵛ: μένειν; Banduri (p. 948): μέν.

continue to do so.[32] Remain steadfast, true [followers] of God, by avoiding and loathing those other doctrines that are opposed to the truth, and those fabrications (fol. 102ʳ) of Beccus. Avoid not only him, but those individuals mentioned above by name who together with him spew out blasphemies which, till now, they have made their own, and which they accept unrepentantly. By so doing, the Paraclete will abide in you,[33] and will preserve you not only from the plague of such error, but from the greater plague of the passions for the participation in the eternal benefits and the blessedness prepared for the just. And may you be and remain so.

The recorded resolution and decision has now been issued by the Church against those who have rebelled and repudiated the Church. In a short while it will be proclaimed by the supreme Judge, unless, before the arrival of His great and manifest day,[34] they set themselves free by repentance, tears and mourning beyond endurance. [246 a-B] For if they repent and look again at the light of Mother Church with the pure eyes of the soul, they will be like those who, in coming to Christ, will not be turned out. To the contrary, Christ will approach the returning one (fol. 102ᵛ) and will embrace him, even if he is a prodigal son who has wasted his in-

[32]Paris. Gr. 1301, fol. 101ᵛ: καὶ ὅσοι τὸ μετὰ ταῦτα τελοῦσιν; Banduri (p. 948): omits the phrase.

[33]Paris. Gr. 1301, fol. 101ʳ: ὑμῖν; Banduri (p. 948): ἡμῖν.

[34]Acts 2:21: "The sun shall be turned into darkness and the moon into blood, before the day of the Lord comes, the great and manifest day."

herited portion,[35] or a lost sheep which had abandoned its sheepfold, or an individual who has removed himself from grace. So it is with the Church which in like manner shall gather them together and reckon as its own and forthwith establish them among the ranks and company of its children, provided they lament one day and experience what we experience now. And although we excommunicate them, separate them from the Church of the devout, impose on them the awesome and great judgment of separation and estrangement from the Orthodox, we do not do it because we wish to exult over their misfortune or to rejoice over their rejection. On the contrary, we grieve and bear their isolation with loathing. But why do we need to act in this fashion? Mainly for two reasons: the first being that their unhappiness and bitterness will cause them, after they have realized their folly, to return repentant and save themselves in the Church. Secondly, others will henceforth be chastened and disciplined so as not to attempt anything similar, or attack that which is holy, or behave willfully against that which is sacred; lest, if they show such audacity, they receive the same rewards in accordance with the example that has been set.

References:

Banduri, A. *Imperium Orientale sive Antiquitates Constantinopolitanae*, I-II (Paris, 1711). The text of the *Tomus* is reprinted in Migne, *PG*.

---

[35]Luke 15:11-32.

RECOMMENDED READING

Carlton, Clark. *The Faith: Understanding Orthodox Christianity*. Salisbury, MA: Regina Orthodox Press, 1997.

Lossky, Vladimir. *The Mystical Theology of the Orthodox Church*. Crestwood, NY: St. Vladimir's Seminary Press, 1976.

Maximovitch, St. John. *The Orthodox Veneration of Mary the Birthgiver of God*. Tr. by Seraphim Rose. Platina, CA: St. Herman of Alaska Brotherhood, 1994.

Meyendorff, John. *Byzantine Theology: Historical Trends and Doctrinal Themes*. New York: Fordham University Press, 1983.

Meyendorff, Afanassieff, Schmemann, and Koulomzine. *The Primacy of Peter*. Bedfordshire: The Faith Press, 1973 (Since republished by SVS Press).

Papadakis, Aristeides. *The Christian East and the Rise of the Papacy: The Church 1071-1453 A.D.* Crestwood, NY: St. Vladimir's Seminary Press, 1994.

Pelikan, Jaroslav. *The Christian Tradition: A history of the Development of Doctrine*. 5 Vols. Chicago: University of Chicago Press, 1971-1989).

Pomazansky, Michael. *Orthodox Dogmatic Theology: A Concise Exposition*. Tr. by Seraphim Rose. Platina, CA: St. Herman of Alaska Brotherhood, 1994.

Pulcini, Theodore. *Orthodoxy and Catholicism: What are the Differneces?* Ben Lomond, CA: Conciliar Press, 1995.

Romanides, John. *Franks, Romans, Feudalism and Doctrine.* Brookline, MA: Holy Cross Orthodox Press, 1981.

Rose, Seraphim. The Place of Blessed Augustine in the Orthodox Church. Platina, CA: St. Herman of Alaska Brotherhood, 1983.

Ware, Kallistos. *The Orthodox Way.* Crestwood, NY: St. Vladimir's Seminary Press, 1995.

Vasileios, Archimandrite. *Hymn of Entry: Liturgy and Life in the Orthodox Church.* Tr. by Elizabeth Briere. Crestwood, NY: St. Vladimir's Seminary Press, 1984.

Vlachos, Hierotheos. *The Mind of the Orthodox Church.* Tr. by Esther Williams. Levadia, Greece: Birth of the Theotokos Monastery, 1998.

Whelton, Michael. *Two Paths: Papal Monarchy – Collegial Tradition.* Salisbury, MA: Regina Orthodox Press, 1998.

Young, Alexey. *The Rush to Embrace.* Richfield Springs, NY: Nikodemos Orthodox Publication Society, 1996.

Zizioulas, John. *Being as Communion: Studies in Personhood and the Church.* Crestwood, NY: St. Vladimir's Seminary Press, 1985.

MORE FROM REGINA ORTHODOX PRESS
CHECK OR CREDIT CARD INFO A <u>MUST!</u>

BUY 5 ITEMS OR MORE *SAVE 40%* ON

BOOKS/BIBLES

#_____	THE TRUTH	$22.95
#_____	THE THIRD MILLENNIUM BIBLE	$45.00
#_____	THE NON ORTHODOX	$19.95
#_____	TWO PATHS	$22.95
#_____	THE SCANDAL OF GENDER	$22.95
#_____	ETERNAL DAY	$22.95
#_____	THE FAITH	$22.95
#_____	THE WAY	$22.95
#_____	DANCING ALONE	$20.00

CD ROM'S

#_____	HOLY WEEK	$45.00
#_____	PILGRIMAGE TO MT ATHOS	$45.00

VIDEO TAPES

#_____	THE DEFENSE OF ORTHODOXY	$59.85
#_____	ORTHODOX EVANGELISM	$29.95
#_____	PERSONAL JOURNEY - ORTHODOXY	$19.95
#_____	TRUE STATE OF THE UNION	$19.95

MUSIC CD'S

#_____	GATES OF REPENTANCE	$19.95
#_____	FIRST FRUITS	$19.95
Subtotal		$_____
MA residents add 5% sales tax		$_____

BUY 5 ITEMS OR MORE *SUBTRACT 40%* $_____

Add 10% for shipping (Non-USA 20%) $_____

GRAND TOTAL $_____

NAME _____

ADDRESS _____

CITY _____

STATE _____ ZIP _____

E-MAIL _____

PHONE _____

MC or VISA # _____ exp. _____

SIGNATURE _____

REGINA ORTHODOX PRESS PO BOX 5288 SALISBURY MA 01952 USA

TOLL FREE 800 636 2470 Fax 978 462 5079 non-USA 978 463 0730 \

QUESTIONS??? www.reginaorthodoxpress.com